ETCETERA **etc.**

creating beautiful interiors with
the things you love.

ETCETERA **etc.**
creating beautiful interiors with
the things you love.
~Sibella Court~

PHOTOGRAPHY BY CHRIS COURT

MURDOCH BOOKS

CONTENTS

ME
I think in point form
I see in still life
I am a collector of all things beautiful
I am a list-maker, shopper and beachcomber
I observe everything and rarely miss a detail
I am a shop owner
A designer of paint colours
An interior stylist

INTRODUCTION

THIS BOOK IS ABOUT SLAPDASH STYLING AND DECONSTRUCTED
DECORATING SOLUTIONS. IT'S FILLED WITH THINGS THAT INSPIRE
ME AND MAY IN TURN EXCITE YOU OR TRIGGER IDEAS FOR YOUR
OWN HOME. MY HOPE IS THAT WHEN YOU FLICK THROUGH THE
PAGES YOU'LL BEGIN TO LOOK AT YOUR POSSESSIONS FROM A NEW
PERSPECTIVE AND BE ENCOURAGED TO CONFIDENTLY RESHUFFLE,
PIN, PAINT, PASTE, SCRIBBLE, AND ORGANISE YOUR INTERIORS
SO THEY FEEL ALL SHINY AND NEW (EVEN IF ALL YOU LOVE IS
WEATHERED AND OLD!).

Each chapter is brimming with trade secrets I picked up in my
years as a stylist working on photo shoots in studios, building
sets and still lives from scratch, or on location in hotels,
shops, restaurants and clubs, and other people's living and private
spaces. It is also a visual diary of my life as just about every
item in the book — bought, found, old, new, natural and man-made
— comes from my own archives.

To guide you, I have come up with a series of colour palettes
and loose formulas for hunting and gathering, showing and telling,
so that you can have a focus when shopping and sourcing things.
I have only one rule: seek out beauty and meaning in everything,
then embrace and display it. Even the most humble and everyday of
objects can be transformed.

I encourage you to look in unusual places, not just the pages
of magazines. If you open your eyes to nature, history and story
books, music, travel, fashion and textiles, sets in the cinema and
theatre, art, exhibitions, or the ceremonies and customs of other
cultures, then fresh, original ideas will follow.

Please use this book like a journal: tag it, dog ear it, and
write in it with pen; highlight if you must. Save your notes
between my pages and use the images as a reference and guide to
show at your local paint, salvage and hardware stores.

This book is full of simple suggestions for styling your space.
It is not about full-blown, expensive renovations or a directive to
go out buy everything new, it is about becoming the curator of your
own style and the creator of beautiful and evocative interiors.

A PERSONAL MUSEUM

For me, a home is like a museum without the signs saying 'Please Don't Touch'. Think of all the stuff you own that has emotional or historical significance or comes with a memory or tale of where, when and who. It's just a matter of finding ways to incorporate these things into your surroundings as three-dimensional reminders of your life for you and others to experience. This means you'll end up with a home that's distinctly and beautifully yours and not just a replica of homewares catalogues or generic furniture stores. It also allows your living space to evolve over time rather than locking it into a specific era or decorating genre.

My own home is a virtual timeline of my life and loves, places I've travelled and people I've met. Some of my most vivid memories are enmeshed in the vast amounts of fabric I own. My mother, Dee, an Asian textiles expert, nurtured a similar passion in me and nourished me with her intoxicating knowledge of weaving, embroidering and dyeing techniques. Now, everywhere I go I acquire more and more metres, some just because of the way it looks, others because they capture a memory as potent as any photograph.

Another love is sea treasure: coral, pebbles, sea urchins, shells, seaweed, driftwood etc. It reminds me of when I was a little girl. My grandparents owned land around the beautiful Smith's Lake on New South Wales' north coast and we spent every holiday roaming, swimming, walking, sailing, fishing, and combing the shores. Now, I pick up sea miscellany all over the world.

Consider this list, then start to think of the items you own that could tell a similar story:

I love to pick up a perfectly tossed grey stone with a white stripe and be transported to Portofino some time in 1995 drinking a Santa Margherita pinot grigio.

A religious dharma made of shells that was bought on a trip, made on a whim, to Naples after I ran into an ex-boyfriend in Paris.

A nestled stack of six white ceramic scientific bowls, slightly crusty, with no known purpose, but bought (not even haggled for!) at one of my all-time favourite flea markets, Le Marché aux Puces de la Porte de Vanves, Paris. Every adventure to this market would begin with a jamón baguette from the van on the corner.

A crown of dried giant kelp collected for me by a past love and carefully transported from Big Sur, California to New York.

Beeswax still intact in a much-used wooden pane bought from an amused beekeeper who lived in a caravan on the snowy, hilly surrounds of Tashkent, Uzbekistan. It was early spring, the first blossoms were out and children were selling tiny early tulips, so delicate and fragile.

My grandmother's treasures: shells we do not see on our shores any more, jet beads, tiny seed pearls in an old department store box, handmade sandwich signs about one and half inches high saying 'watercress' and 'devilled egg', silver napkin rings.

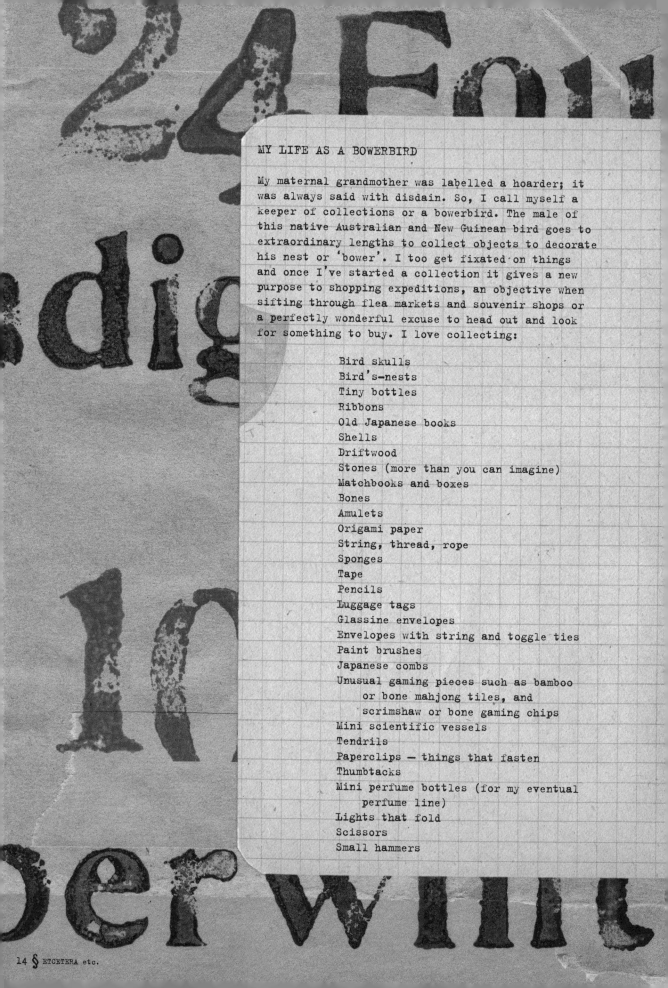

MY LIFE AS A BOWERBIRD

My maternal grandmother was labelled a hoarder; it was always said with disdain. So, I call myself a keeper of collections or a bowerbird. The male of this native Australian and New Guinean bird goes to extraordinary lengths to collect objects to decorate his nest or 'bower'. I too get fixated on things and once I've started a collection it gives a new purpose to shopping expeditions, an objective when sifting through flea markets and souvenir shops or a perfectly wonderful excuse to head out and look for something to buy. I love collecting:

Bird skulls
Bird's-nests
Tiny bottles
Ribbons
Old Japanese books
Shells
Driftwood
Stones (more than you can imagine)
Matchbooks and boxes
Bones
Amulets
Origami paper
String, thread, rope
Sponges
Tape
Pencils
Luggage tags
Glassine envelopes
Envelopes with string and toggle ties
Paint brushes
Japanese combs
Unusual gaming pieces such as bamboo
        or bone mahjong tiles, and
            scrimshaw or bone gaming chips
Mini scientific vessels
Tendrils
Paperclips — things that fasten
Thumbtacks
Mini perfume bottles (for my eventual
        perfume line)
Lights that fold
Scissors
Small hammers

I have a lot of stuff (yes, I really am just a
good old-fashioned hoarder like my grandmother!)
so I've built floor-to-ceiling shelves to house
it all. They've become my cabinets, or shelves,
of curiosity. Corners to explore, study and enjoy.
You can do this too, anywhere you like — on window
sills, mantels and dressing tables. Line things up
on a baseboard on the floor or hang textiles from
a suspended pole from the ceiling. Do not limit
yourself with display and let your collections speak
for themselves depending on their format and shape.

THE

THE

SOCIETY
INC

S O C I E T Y
INC

The Society Inc. is my haberdashery meets hardware
store with some other intriguing and exquisite
objects added for the sheer joy of them. It was
named to reflect my fascination with old clubs and
societies devoted to specific causes or ideologies.
To match my short attention span and constant need
for change, the products for sale at The Society
Inc. are changed each season. Each year there are
four distinct themes or 'societies' unified by
a textural and colour palette — which includes a
Society Inc. paint range — and a loose historical,
cultural and nature-based framework. The chapters
in this book are based on five of those themes.

For all the dimensions available to look at in the world, colour is one of the most captivating. In my job as a stylist, a 10-Colour-Palette has evolved as the best starting point for decorating a space. This palette gives me positive boundaries to work with and, whether I use two, four, six or all of the colours, allows me to play with the mood of a room or house and ensures a unified end result.

To help illustrate the mindset I follow when creating such a palette, I have divided this book into five chapters — Foundation, Indigo Blues, Travellers & Magicians, Paperwhites, and Tradewinds — each anchored by 10 colours. If you love my colours, feel free to use them as your own, but creating your own 10-Colour-Palette is as easy as walking around your house and pinpointing things you already own and love. It might be a beautiful porcelain bowl, a postcard, a cocktail ring, an embroidered tablecloth inherited from your grandmother, or the print on your favourite dress. Consider everything: jewellery, clothes, food, garden flora and fauna, photographs, anything made with fabric or paper, solid colours and patterns, silverware and ceramics, art, buttons, ribbons and trims.

Nature, in particular, should be a major of source of inspiration as it reveals natural colour combinations and textures that rarely disappoint. I once did a photoshoot based entirely around the colours of a monarch butterfly: Damascus red, mustard and ochre oranges, and dirty cream. I pick up feathers, leaves, flowers, rocks and tree branches. Now it's your turn to observe nature in the same way.

Next, start looking beyond your immediate surroundings, especially at things that don't have an interior design purpose, and make a note of what appeals to you. It could be the falling-off-label on an old bottle, a swizzle stick, an crusty street lamp, coins, a weathered shop sign, a discarded playing card, wooden toys, a faded wall of graffiti, silvery puddles on rainy days, crumbly slate from an old roof, a finely-etched tumbler, crunchy white linen, just-poured cement, thick mothy felt, or a scene from a favourite movie or novel. Take photos, make notes, and start acquiring.

Soon it will become obvious that you are attracted to similar things over and over again and it's time to start playing. Put together a selection of pieces you've collected and see what kind of colour palette reveals itself. Add and subtract until it takes on a visual order. There are no right or wrong combinations because it is your interior and it's a matter of finding what makes you happy. Most of the time a harmonious palette is achieved, one that will become the basis for future decorating and shopping adventures. Remember, you will be able to use the colours in varying combinations. Some rooms will be quiet and subtle, utilising the softer, more neutral tones. Others will be louder, denser in colour, pattern and texture.

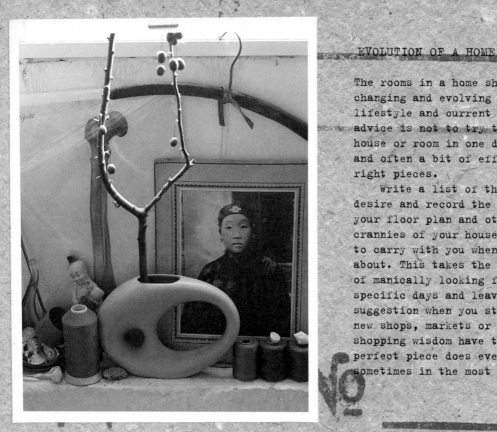

EVOLUTION OF A HOME

The rooms in a home should be forever changing and evolving to suit your mood, lifestyle and current obsessions, so my advice is not to try to decorate a whole house or room in one day. It takes time and often a bit of effort to find the right pieces.

Write a list of things you need or desire and record the measurements of your floor plan and other nooks and crannies of your house in a notebook to carry with you when you're out and about. This takes the pressure out of manically looking for objects on specific days and leaves you open to suggestion when you stumble across new shops, markets or sales. Years of shopping wisdom have taught me that your perfect piece does eventually turn up, sometimes in the most unexpected places.

ROOMS WITH A VIEW

Before you start transforming a space, view it from every vantage point and at a few times of the day. Stop and notice what you see when you enter, sit on the furniture, stand in corners, walk around the room, turn lights on and off, and open and shut the doors. Take particular note of transitional areas such as the hallways and the way in which doorways frame the spaces beyond. This is your opportunity to create depth and layers, to consider places to hang unusual textiles, use splashes of colour or a random piece of furniture, or a new window treatment. Walls may need an interest point, whether it's wallpaper or some form of art. Ceilings could need a pendant light or mobile. A small room may benefit from a solid splash of colour and a full-length mirror, a large space from a floor treatment. Make every object count.

samarkand

oasis

absinthe

aral sea

natura morta

attar of rose

paperbag

tanguy

porcelain

THE POWER OF PAINT

I love paint. I love its immediacy. I love being able to choose eco-friendly options with a range of interesting finishes. I love that you can do it yourself and that you can completely overhaul, renew, or refresh a space in an afternoon's work.

When you flick through the pages of this book and see a paint colour or application you like, follow these guidelines before you begin and you'll end up with a rewarding result.

Swatch, swatch, swatch: Visit the local hardware or paint store and buy small pots of a few colours that you like — don't be scared to try something new — or those that fit in your 10-Colour-Palette. If the choice is there, get an assortment of different finishes: matt, semi and full gloss, and metallic are just some of the options available.

Take your selection home and paint large swatches, about one metre (or two feet) square, in various parts of the room. Study the results at different times of the day, in natural and artificial light. This is very important as the appearance of a paint colour can change depending on the size and orientation of the room, colours and spatial elements — furniture and art for example — by which it's surrounded.

Alternatively, paint your desired colours on large one metre squares of pure white paper and tape them to various spots on your walls. Be aware that finish and colour can be slightly altered when painting on paper, but this is a great solution if you want to explore painting options for a number of rooms in your home but are not yet ready to begin.

Look at your swatches for at least 24 hours before you make your decisions.

Once you begin painting, don't worry if you can't achieve a professional finish. Some colours look great when they're slightly uneven as it gives it a more tactile feel. And remember, if you don't like it or you really do a botched job, you can paint over the top and start again.

ARCANE
TRADES

falconer etc.

ARCANE TRADES

No. 10

No. 9

No. 8

No. 7

No. 6

No. 5

No. 4

No. 3

No. 2

No. 1

Archer
Boatbuilder
Saddler
Innkeeper
Bonesetter
Book peddler
Ship chandler
Iron forger
Chimney sweep
Fishmonger
Cobbler
Stonecutter
Merchant
Beekeeper
Mapmaker
Riverkeeper
Mask carver
Fan maker

falconer etc.

YOUR TOOLKIT

A hot glue gun will fix and fasten most things.

Adhesive putty, commonly known by the brand name Blu-Tack, can be a cheap alternative to framing. Use it for sticking up all your ephemera.

Do not disregard rough edges, selvedges, things that are skewed or wonky or even broken, the backs of things (or, as I like to call it, side B), fraying, uneven paint jobs, non-treated surfaces.

Look out for old or vintage hardware, such as hooks, curtain rings, clips and clasps, nails, and tacks, and you'll find lovely and distinct shapes that are unavailable today.

Sewing notions such as thread and cotton, ribbon, scissors, safety and dressmakers' pins for hanging, displaying and mending.

Check out salvage shops, car-boot sales, flea markets and garage sales, especially if you're away from home or in another country.

All sorts of pens, chalk, paint pens, and pencils for marking and writing on any surface.

All kinds of tape, especially blue 3M-brand tape (it's effortlessly removable), brown paper tape and masking tape in all its widths. I use all of these regularly and for all sorts of purposes: hanging maps on walls, holding pictures in frames or securing paper bunting over a doorway. Velcro and 3M-brand hanging products attach so many things.

Learn to use spackle and sandpaper to make changes or fix mistakes.

Make friends with tradesmen. Encourage them to do different things.

Learn how to drill and plug a hole in the wall so you don't have to wait for someone else to do it. Buy picture-rail hooks, string, wire, sharp skinny brass hanging tacks (they are unobtrusive and easily removed), and all kinds of nails. Play with the placement of your pieces on the wall to achieve the right scale and positioning.

A small, handbag-sized notebook for measurements, reminders and lists. I like Moleskin and Muji brands.

Tape measures: a lightweight 150 cm (60 in) one that's always in your bag, plus a sturdy, retractable 5 m (5 yds) one.

Digital or phone cameras are a must for shopping trips. Always ask the shop keeper before you start snapping stuff in the store. Photograph the shop's business card or window as a reminder.

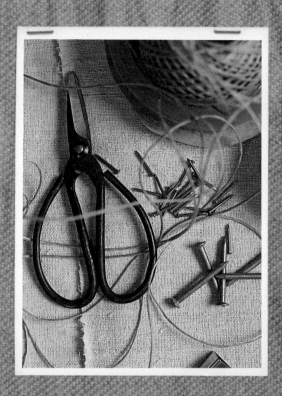

DEDICATION

My mother specialised in Islamic textiles
from Central Asia. She travelled the world
to find out all she could about textiles and
she instilled a similar passion in me. She
died in 2008 in a desert camp in Rajasthan,
India, doing the things she loved best.
Her final textile was the paranja, a woven
horsehair veil, edged in indigo, worn as a
head covering by Islamic women in Central
Asia. She tracked down the last remaining
gypsy who knew how to weave one and had a
lesson in its unique technique. I dedicate
this book to her.

styl·ist - noun

a designer or consultant in a field subject
to changes in style, esp. fashion or
interior decoration.

a person who cultivates or maintains any
particular style; one who adds style.

a finder, keeper and curator of
beautiful objects.

GRAVE ST WHARF
TRAL BAY JUNCT
TRAL BAY WHARF
RTH BALGOWLAH
RTHBRIDGE
RTHBRIDGE JUNCT
RTH
TH SYD
N CH
SBORNE
ACECO
ILWAY
AILWA
DAN AND
1

Foundation

01

foun·da·tion – noun

the basis or groundwork of anything: the moral foundation of both society and religion.

the natural or prepared ground or base on which some structure rests.

the lowest division of a building, wall, or the like, usually of masonry and partly or wholly below the surface of the ground.

№ 1	**Pirate black**
№ 2	**Cracked leather**
№ 3	**Paperbag**
№ 4	**Burlap**
№ 5	**Gypsy gold**
№ 6	**Felt**
№ 7	**Sailcloth**
№ 8	**Scrimshaw**
№ 9	**Chalk**
№ 10	**Glassine**

EVERY ONE OF MY 10-COLOUR-PALETTES COMES WITH A STORY, A
ONCE-UPON-A-TIME OF THE WAY IN WHICH THE PALETTE CAME TO BE.
FOUNDATION IS NO EXCEPTION — THE FOLLOWING PAGES ARE FILLED
WITH TALES AND TRAPPINGS FROM MY LIFE'S ADVENTURES. BUT, THIS
CHAPTER SERVES ANOTHER, MORE PRACTICAL, PURPOSE. FOUNDATION
IS AS ITS TITLE SUGGESTS: A SOLID COLOUR BASE FOR ANY INTERIOR.
IF YOU'RE A GARDENER, CONSIDER IT THE FERTILE SOIL, SUNSHINE
AND RAIN; IF YOU'RE A COOK, THINK OF IT AS THE FLOUR, EGGS,
AND SUGAR. WITH THE RIGHT FOUNDATIONS, ANYTHING IS POSSIBLE.

BUILDING YOUR SET

The theatre is a wonderful place for a stylist like me. Aside
from all the obvious appeal of the acting, drama, music, and dance,
the set design offers so many ideas. I love to watch the sets
change before my eyes: one minute the action's in a house, the next
by the sea, but all on the same stage. I like to think of my home
and shop in the same way, with each room providing the backdrop
for my latest obsessions or ever-changing needs and wants. But
while some of us revel in the thought of frequent floor-to-ceiling
transformations, others like to take a more low-risk approach by
leaving the basics or the big-ticket items (the walls, carpets,
light fixtures, furniture and window coverings) and changing the
less permanent features when the styling urge takes over.
    Foundation is a 10-Colour-Palette designed to be built upon,
a beautifully neutral set of colours that literally goes with
anything. All the colours complement, anchor, embrace or accent
the colours in all the other chapters in the book. Paint your
bedroom in a Foundation colour and dress it up with the vivid hues
of Travellers & Magicians. Buy the lounge you've always coveted in
a Foundation colour then scatter it with cushions inspired by the
Indigo Blues. Lay a Foundation-coloured carpet and the fairytale
charm of Paperwhites can follow. Let Foundation be your basics,
Tradewinds your personal added extras.

POCKET-MONEY STYLE

While Foundation has the benefit of working well in any space and within many aesthetics, it is also a complete and beautifully refined option on its own. Open my wardrobe and you'll find just about everything is a shade of white, cream and caramel. Look at the constants on my favourite-things lists and you'll see string, scrimshaw, sailcloth, cracked leather, gypsies' earrings and coins much fondled and many times counted, burlap and hessian, old metal fixtures, film and stamps in paper glassine envelopes, and, above all else, brown paper. Brown paper self-striped, tied up with string, pattern-making paper, boxes, grocery bags and sandwich bags. All of them are neutral-coloured.

The other thing about this list is its humble origins. Nothing here is rarefied or expensive; everything is easy to find and mostly practical in use. Look at the styling ideas I've used to display these collectibles and curiosities and you'll see that you don't need a whopping cheque book or an educated eye for art and architecture to begin creating an interior style for your home. Keep your mind open to all the possibilities.

THE LOGIC OF WOOD

The influence of nature is apparent in all my palettes but in Foundation it is wood that soars. It's not quite that I see a tree and imagine it as a chair. It's more that in just about every natural landscape, whether on the coast or in the desert, in a rainforest or the park down the road, it's easy to find a tree and observe it as part of nature's unparalleled colour palette and borrow its natural pairings.

Also, in the home, it's difficult to go wrong with things made of wood. No matter what its origin (pine, oak, blackwood, jarrah) or use (chairs, tables, picture frames, bowls, or boxes) it is a very adaptable, durable and attractive choice. Look for objects that highlight its grain, colour and texture; buy items with the hallmarks of age; consider pieces you can gently restore, renew or mend. Reinvent broken pieces, too.

IN THE KNOW

In any one week, a stylist can be a builder, artist, upholsterer, framer, cook, seamstress, narrator, calligrapher, carpenter, photographer's assistant — even a model. Every new shoot I do sends me down the path of a new trade and every new theme I embark on opens a field of expertise. When it comes to your own interior decorating, it pays to do the same, as these skills too are the foundations of styling. Read books, search the internet, interrogate tradesmen and talented friends. Learn to hang a picture and thread a sewing machine, discover the nuances of different paint finishes and adhesives, perfect stain removal for second-hand fabrics. The more adept you are with a hammer, nails and paintbrush, the more you'll have to spend on the things you love.

Many people would not take a second look at forgotten or superseded hardware such as this, but for me it holds as much wonder as a treasure chest. The spectrum of colours that springs from a basic mix of ageing wood and tarnished metal is a perfect illustration of my Foundation colours. It offers unusual alternatives for hanging or displaying things around the home: brass hooks, curtain rings, handmade wooden pegs, string and electrical cord, iron nails, brown paper tape, steel ship pulleys and shackles, and rubber bands.

Humble, everyday items — lead pencils sharpened with knives — are especially appealing to me. I wrote the first draft of this book in pencil while sitting on the beach.

The Society inc.

18 Stewart street Paddington NSW 2021
tel/fax: (02) 9331 1592

Your home is not a showroom and a
mixture of furniture from all eras is
perfectly acceptable, especially when
anchored by similar colours or shapes
or the mere notion that you love it.

Paper luggage tags, from the local
newsagent or stationer, are one of the
most useful things you can buy. Tie
them with string, ribbon or pins and
use them as cards, for labelling
drawers, jotting down notes, anything
you can think of.

A little sticky putty plus
an instant art installat
through your own draw
for invitations, cards a
start a collection from
matter such as sewing
loveletters made interest
or desirable by the idios

lot of paper equals
. Begin by rummaging
s and storage boxes
other memorabilia or
ratch. Seek out printed
tterns, maps, flashcards or
g by the passage of time
crasies of the paper itself.

This scrappy paper napkin
scribbled with a sentimental
farewell note and casually placed
on a table offers an unexpected
alternative to the usual photo
memorabilia.

Transparent, crackly glassine
envelopes are one of many examples
of the diversity of paper. Type on
it, frame it, use it as place
cards for your next dinner party.

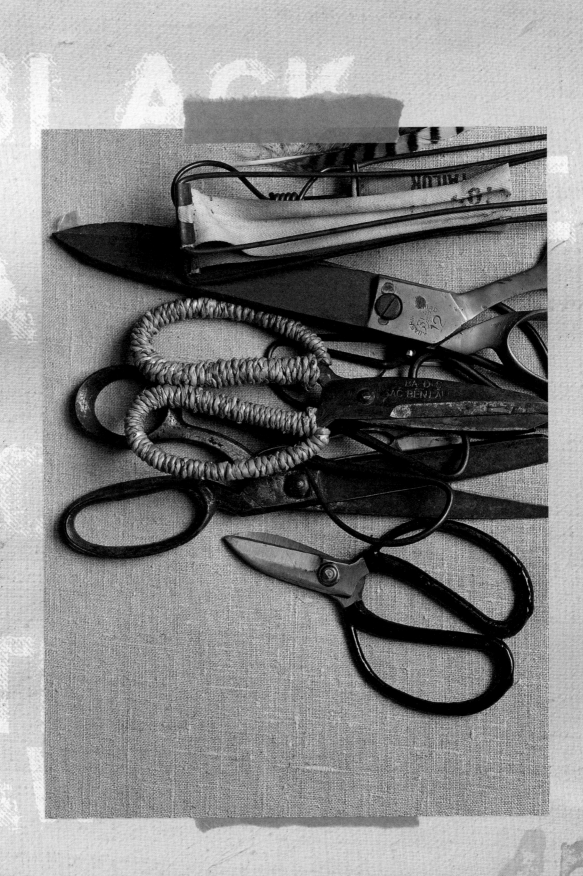

36, 4

[PREVIOUS PAGE]

Three base colours and a loose
equine theme give this mantel
display a photo-perfect,
still-life quality. Note the
variations in scale and shape
to stimulate the eye.

Consider not just the objects
themselves but the way they meld
in with their surroundings. This
improvised sculpture of rusted
barbed wire (could art cost any
less?) casts curious shadows on
the wall.

Stacked empty frames act as display blocks and a background for random found objects, both man-made and natural. Glass items, such as the dome, give a whole new perspective to the objects behind and allow you to arrange and view multiple layers.

Turn bookcases into display cases for just about anything you own. A hat collection, set out and ready to wear, is a practical storage solution but is equally compelling for the repetition of similar shapes and textures.

Do not overlook random finds from your weekend bushwalk. Shivery grass, abandoned wasp nests, and part of a snake vertebra sit beautifully in installation.

Affix light objects to the wall using removable adhesive hooks, or permanent ones, and change the vignette when the mood takes you.

PRIVATE PROP[ERTY]

Positively *No* Tressp[assing]

Under Penalty of

5 7

Old signs act as a humorous distraction from everyday household items such as a functional storage cupboard.

Using words as decoration allows you to introduce a true sense of self to your interiors. This old lampshade has been customised with a bedtime phrase, but you could pen a nursery rhyme, poem or a favourite saying.

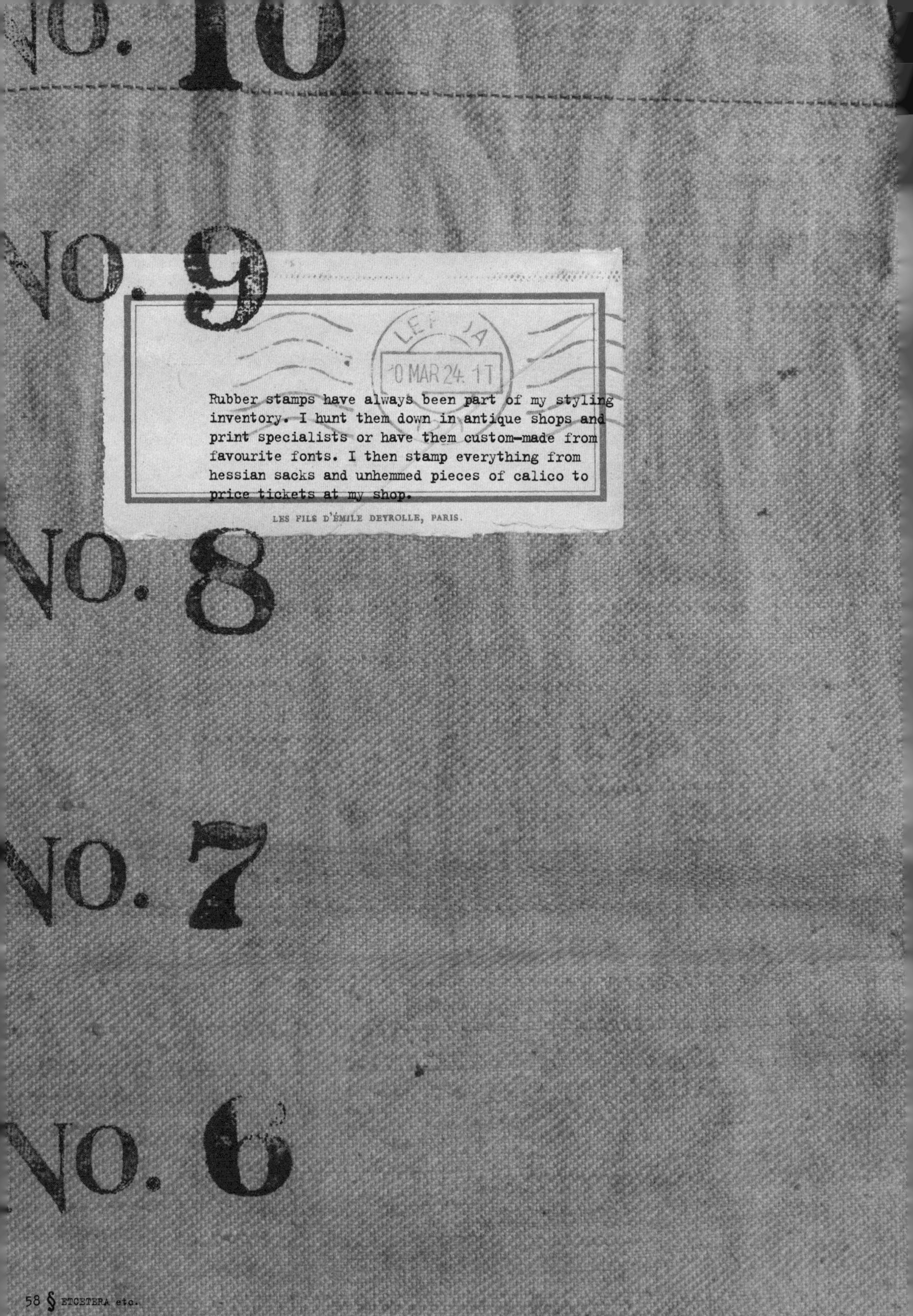

NO. 10

NO. 9

Rubber stamps have always been part of my styling
inventory. I hunt them down in antique shops and
print specialists or have them custom-made from
favourite fonts. I then stamp everything from
hessian sacks and unhemmed pieces of calico to
price tickets at my shop.

LES FILS D'ÉMILE DEYROLLE, PARIS.

NO. 8

NO. 7

NO. 6

1860
ab

From: The Society inc.
        18 Stewart Street
        Paddington NSW 2021
        AUSTRALIA

Museums and historic houses are a constant source of stimulation for me, and not just for the history lessons I receive. I love the exhibits that re-create rooms and capture moments in time — the servants' quarters, the butler's pantry, an indoor swimming pool circa 1900 — and come home filled with new styling and shopping ideas. I bought an old-fashioned typewriter for its font and printing inconsistencies but like the reaction it gets from friends remembering the days before computers.

Crunchy starched linen found on the roll is the perfect width for curtain panels. Buy a metre (3.3 feet) longer than the drop of your window and allow it to cascade and pool on the floor. Use a brass kilt pin as a tie back. Invest in trestle or occasional tables that can be moved about to suit both your decorative and practical needs.

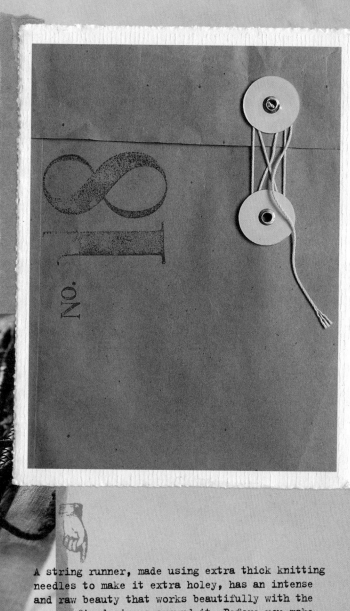

NO. 181

A string runner, made using extra thick knitting needles to make it extra holey, has an intense and raw beauty that works beautifully with the more refined pieces around it. Before you make your next interior purchase, close your eyes and touch it. Consider its weight, texture, shape and size and match it with the opposite.

Pick a theme and run with it: the zebra-patterned linen on the cover of 'I Married Adventure', a braided leather whip and a photograph of an elephant reflect the neutral palette of colonial safari-wear.

What more is there to say about brown paper packages except that I just can't let go of a time of hand-penned, stamped and posted correspondence and the adventures and stories immortalised on the pages within.

GRANVILLE METHO

Back Row: G. Alton
2nd Row: H. McCole, F. McCabe, F. Smith, E. Otter, W. Hodges
3rd Row: G. Ahbarch, F. Perry, G. Healey, J. Rogers, G. McCloer, E. Singer
4th Row: Mr. Perry (V. Pres.), F. White, A. E. Haigh (Organiser), S. Lands, Mr. J
Front Row: J. Pott, M. Pearce, F. Rabson, T. G.

御馬上の御尊影

宮内省御写真版下

Old metal fringing
Cut velvet, slightly threadbare,
    in deep greens & Damascus reds
Burlap covered seats
Oversized papier maché props
Giant clamshells
Animal costumes
Parts of sets
Old windows
Pots of paint
Random chairs
Faux rocks & boulders
Gates
Masks
Painted fire buckets
Dyed ostrich feathers
Bear rugs
Heavy netting
Swords & daggers

PARAPHERNALIA
FOUND
BACKSTAGE
AT THE BALLET
RUSSES

Giant keys
Discarded crowns & turbans
Glass beads of all colours
Silk cord
Thick, greasy face paint
Brocade curtains

lion statues etc.

Old metal fringing
Cut velvet, slightly threadbare,
in deep greens & Damascus reds
Burlap covered seats
Oversized papier mache props
Giant clamshells
Animal costumes
Parts of sets
Old windows
Pots of paint
Random chairs
Faux rocks & boulders
Gates
Masks
Painted fire buckets
Dyed ostrich feathers
Bear rugs
Heavy netting
Swords & daggers

PARAPHERNALIA
FOUND
BACKSTAGE
AT THE BALLET
RUSSES

Giant keys
Discarded crowns & turbans
Glass beads of all colours
Silk cord
Thick, greasy face paint
Brocade curtains

lion statues etc.

Bring a level of authenticity to your interiors by sourcing old hardware such as slightly rusting nails, screws and hooks. Maybe your grandfather has an assorted jarful in his back shed. Then, if you have a fetish for fashion, display your wares for all the world to see.

An old brass light switch found at a salvage shop makes an interesting change from the modern, mass-produced versions.

THE

Abandon precise and measured hanging
arrangements in favour of a dense, off-kilter
grouping. Add new acquisitions as you go.

Chalkboards and chalkboard paint (which comes in
many colours) splashed on a wall offer transient
and thoughtful design opportunities. Write your
favourite quotes or just make a things-to-do list.

[NEXT PAGE]

Wrapping art around walls, or placing it
asymmetrically or at different heights instantly
changes the focal point of a space.

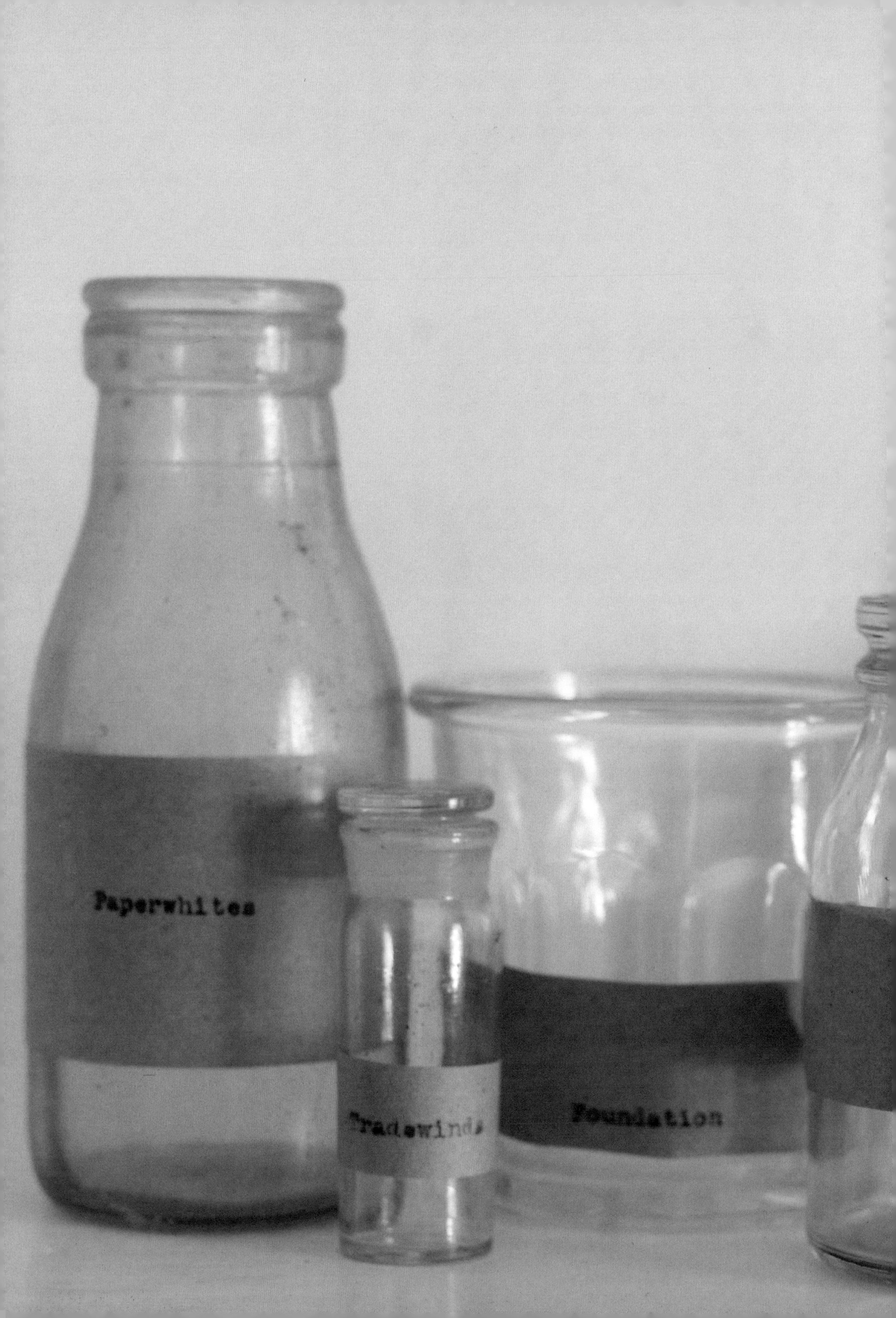
Paperwhites
Tradewinds
Foundation

Everyday glass jars get a
makeover with stamped brown
paper cuffs. Keep them empty
or fill them with flowers
or collectibles.

digo Blues

Travellers
&
Magicians

Indigo Blues

02

in·di·go — adjective

a blue dye obtained from
various plants, esp. of
the genus Indigofera, or
manufactured synthetically.

a colour ranging from a deep
violet blue to a dark,
greyish blue.

blue — noun

the pure colour of a clear sky;
the primary colour between green
and violet in the visible
spectrum, an effect of light
with a wavelength between 450
and 500 nm.

№.1   Indigo

№.2   Boro #2

№.3   Boro #1

№.4   Oyster grey

№.5   Shabori

№.6   Tarnished silver

№.7   Soft pewter

№.8   Singing stones

№.9   Ramie

№.10   Porcelain

FOR A LONG TIME I'VE BEEN IN LOVE WITH THE SONG 'INDIGO BLUES' BY LLORCA. THERE'S ONE LINE IN IT WHICH MAKES ME SMILE AND SING ALONG EVERY TIME — 'SMOKIN', DRINKIN', NEVER THINKIN' BLUES' — AND THE TITLE GIVES ME ONE MORE EXCUSE TO BE OBSESSED WITH THE COLOUR OF THE SAME NAME.

THE ORIGIN OF INDIGO

Call it serendipity or simple coincidence, but it seems just about every colour to which I'm drawn has a textile alter-ego. Indigo textiles have origins rooted in the ancient times of many Asian countries, in particular Japan, as indigo dyes from the flower of several species of plant were one of the easiest to source and most inexpensive natural colourings available. My favourite of these are Boro, the repeatedly mended rags worn or used for bedding by rural peasants in Japan. Often heavily stitched and patched, the shades of blue give them a depth and history that is irresistible.

Other favourites are the variations of indigo used in traditional textile printing techniques: the waxy geometric work of Laos; fine batik work from the Miao hill tribes in China; Japanese shibori, the pinpoint precision technique that includes tying, stitching, wrapping and dyeing fabric; and the pleated skirts in rubbed purple-ly indigo of the Thai Dong hill tribe. Then, there's the western version of indigo textiles: good old utilitarian denim. While denim may not be elevated by the craftsmanship of its manufacturing process, the spectrum of blues in each of these is exceptional and worthy of great consideration.

A COLONIAL INFLUENCE

One of my favourite trips was to Hanoi. The people, pace and fragrance of the place are etched in my mind, as are all things visual, in particular the melding of French and Vietnamese sensibilities. This colonial crossover, the result of European settlement in Asia — the English in Hong Kong and India, and the Dutch in Indonesia are other examples — sees the generally vibrant and colourful local aesthetic subdued with more neutral tones to create a superb styling genre all of its own.

So, while the name of this chapter might suggest blue is the one and only, other hues are vital in their ability to change your decorating tempo by making some rooms dynamic and stimulating, others more restrained. For me, linen, which I love in all its forms — crunchy, fine, peasant, oatmeal, bleached, neutral, dyed and starched — is the perfect starting point. I can always find a use for vintage linen from France, the traditional home of linen; thick, heavy and crunchy styles from Belgium; Korean ramie, a very finely woven ancient linen that's translucent and airy; the muslin-like texture of the Japanese version; and coarse, rough and durable homespun from America.

I collect and treasure antique, handcrafted fabrics from all over the world. Those made on a narrow loom, essentially the width of the weaver's body, are particularly lovely. Consider the many ways in which the fabric was used: panels stitched together to make trousseau sheets, artists' smocks, nightdresses, table linen. The individual stitches, whether delicate French hemming or coarse blanket stitch and sometimes the monogram of the sewer, that hold them together reveal a personal style, but are all beautiful in their own right.

THE BEAUTY OF PRE-LOVED

Like all my themes, Indigo Blues is not just about colour but the telling of a story. When you skim the upcoming pages you will learn that I'm a devotee of all things old and often even broken. Give me a second-hand store or an auction over a day at the mall, invite me into your attic or let me loose at a flea market and I'm happy.

My love of pre-loved objects is twofold. First, the patina of age gives so many things — fabric, furniture and paper, tableware and ceramics, wood and metal — unique textural and colour markings. Look at the way a silver tea set tarnishes or the linen on a hardback book fades in the sun. Feel the crumbling paint on a second-hand chair or the smooth handle on an old hammer. These imperfections are hard to mass-produce and the marks of age tell a story of life lived. This is my second reason for being drawn to things of old. I look at the tea-cup stains on a table and wonder what conversations occurred around it. I pick up a discarded leather suitcase from an op-shop and imagine the journeys it's been on. So many stories, so many styling opportunities.

My no-rules rules for table setting: seek out all kinds of fabric — second-hand, offcuts, wondrous new patterns — in your chosen colour palette and throw them on the table like a deconstructed patchwork tablecloth. Embrace imperfection — it doesn't matter if the table shows through or the fabric hangs haphazardly. Offer an assortment of patterned plates and let your guests choose their own. Don't always pick flowers for decoration, use Japanese fortune sticks or poem cards or anything that might offer textural appeal or provoke a conversation.

[PREVIOUS PAGE]

Rethinking your notion of what constitutes wall
art — it's not just frames and canvases — can
have intriguing results. This kimono has been hung
using a length of bamboo tied with twine. Note the
mixture of textures and patterns; soft cushions
are counterbalanced by the wild form of entwined
grapevines, knobbly bamboo stool and timber bench.

Slapdash wallpapering, with all its tracks
and unaligned patterns, creates an eccentric,
transient sculpture.

Look twice at everything in your home, when
foraging at markets, or scouting for souvenirs,
because no matter how inexpensive or seemingly
ordinary, beauty can be found in many things — an
old reel of string or pile of cheap and cheerful
woven bags, for starters.

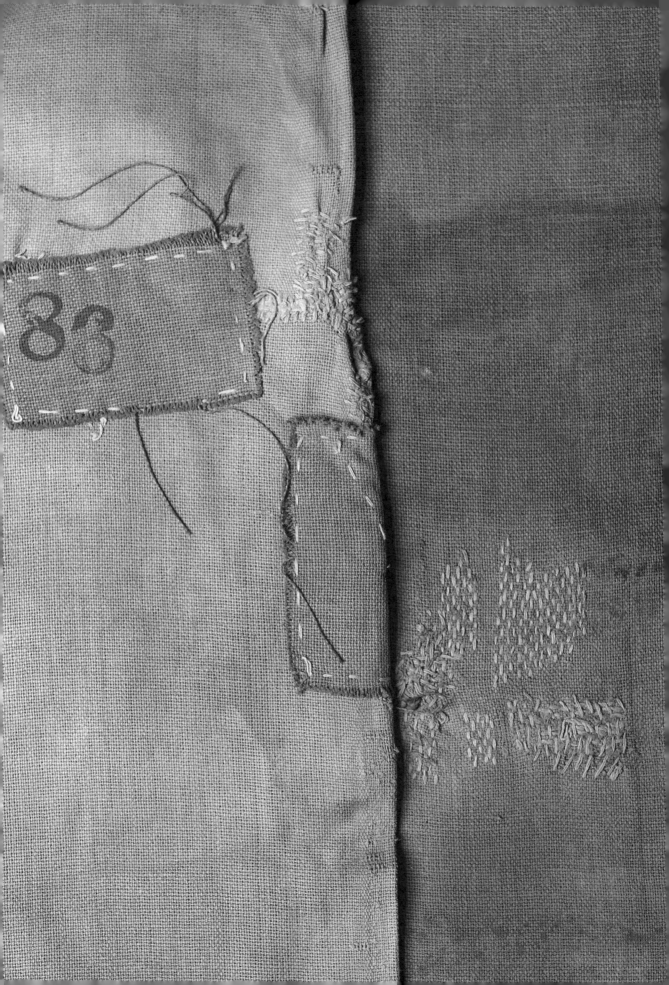

[CONSIDERING HOW MUCH TIME WAS SPENT AT SEA]

Sewing
Tattooing
Birdwatching
Whittling
Scrimshawing
Training pets: monkeys, parrots,
    crickets, dogs
Bone carving: buttons, needles,
    combs, gambling chips
Musical instruments
Knot tying
Making Games: Quoits, balls

SKILLS
THAT SAILORS
HAD OTHER THAN
SAILING

Dancing jigs & singing sea shanties
Reading (most ships had a library)
Basketweaving, and palm and leather
    braiding
Collecting specimens
Botanical drawing/painting
Shooting & skinning animals
Cooking
Herbal remedies
Rope & net making

star gazing etc.

Sewing
Tattooing
Birdwatching
Whittling
Scrimshawing
Training pets: monkeys, parrots,
crickets, dogs
Bone carving: buttons, needles,
combs, gambling chips
Musical instruments
Knot tying
Making Games: Quoits, balls

SKILLS
THAT SAILORS
HAD OTHER THAN
SAILING

Dancing jigs & singing sea shanties
Reading (most ships had a library)
Basketweaving, and palm and leather
braiding
Collecting specimens
Botanical drawing/painting
Shooting & skinning animals
Cooking
Herbal remedies
Rope & net making

star gazing etc.

A couple of years ago while
traveling in Uzbekistan with my
mother, I was lucky to go to a
natural dyeing house/factory in
Bukhara. We looked into the
inky vats and witnessed the
indigo dyeing process and the
finishing step of the dyed
thread drying in the sunshine.

Trade secret: I always have a stash of Blu-Tack
(or other brand of adhesive putty) on styling jobs
or when I'm doing some redecoration as it allows
me to quickly stick things up — postcards, old
theatre tickets, anything on paper — and remove
them without a trace when the mood takes me. Here,
I have tacked inked kimono designs on the wall,
then continued the theme with precise Japanese
calligraphy books — the pages marked and torn by
previous owners.

Ageing imprints beauty onto even the
most humble of man-made objects.
Consider a beached piece of broken boat:
most would see this is as unremarkable
flotsam ready to be discarded, but for
me it has unique textural appeal and its
sculptural qualities pair beautifully
with rough hewn stools next to an
otherwise plain white wall.

Practise your calligraphy on a piece of calico, muslin or linen, then use as a wall piece or table runner.

Bunting — a favourite of mine — is a lovely way to use any fabric swatches you've collected. This one has been sewn from an assortment of vintage Japanese indigo fabric but yours might be fashioned from colours and patterns more suited to a child's room or other favourite place.

There is an extraordinary syn[e...]
interior design and fashion a[...]
a pity to me to hide clothes b[...]
doors. We all have pieces that[...]
whether due to the design of [...]
the reason for its purchase, o[...]
worn. My advice is to do what [...]
the following page with the j[...]
my mum whilst visiting the R[...]
Korea – and display some of yo[...]
for all to see. Note: study fash[...]
interior stylist's eye and you'l[...]
common threads for you to re[...]

y between
so it seems
d closed
a story,
garment,
place it was
ave done on
ket – made for
he festival in
beloved pieces
with an
on discover
oduce at home.

9

One of the cheapest and most rewarding interior design options is paper and paper products. Stationery, envelopes stuffed with old letters, books, souvenir postcards and those bought at art exhibitions, posters, magazines, newspapers in foreign languages... Wherever you go, whether it's the local school fete or a market in a far-flung destination, look for paper in varying textures, weights and colours. Seek out quirky handwritten items and printed matter with unusual fonts and typesetting. When you return home the possibilities will start to present themselves as you begin framing, tacking and hanging them to the walls.

While I'm perfectly content with throwing
things into baskets, filling jars and
inventing other ways of decoratively
displaying my possessions, I'm equally devoted
to finding practical — read neat and tidy
— storage solutions. Look for second-hand
shelving and cabinetry from apothecaries or
industrial filing cabinets and drawers in a
mixture of timber and metal. Note the futon
cover on the floor is lovingly repaired —
which gives it a legacy that cannot be found
in something new.

I'm reluctant to buy anything new if repairing
it myself is an option. When all was creaking
and cracking underfoot I came across lead-
lined stairs with dome shaped tacks in an
old shopping arcade and managed to track down
similar tacks to hammer lead sheets over the
holes in my floorboards.

These indigo-dyed, toed peasant shoes and
the boro on which they sit intrigue me for
their anthropological significance, but, more
importantly, they also help illustrate one of
the many ways to finetune your colour palette.
Look at the gradual and natural fading of the
dye caused through wear and tear and you'll
see beautifully graduated shades of indigo
— any of which you can use.

Faded and falling apart or pre-loved, linen-covered books offer a beautiful colour palette and, when stacked high, also illustrate a display technique used by stylists the world over.

Hand-carved Japanese wood blocks offer tactile appeal.

An oversized Japanese abacus is a unique substitute for a bedhead with layers of Japanese, Laotian and Indian indigo textiles replacing more obvious choices of bed linen.

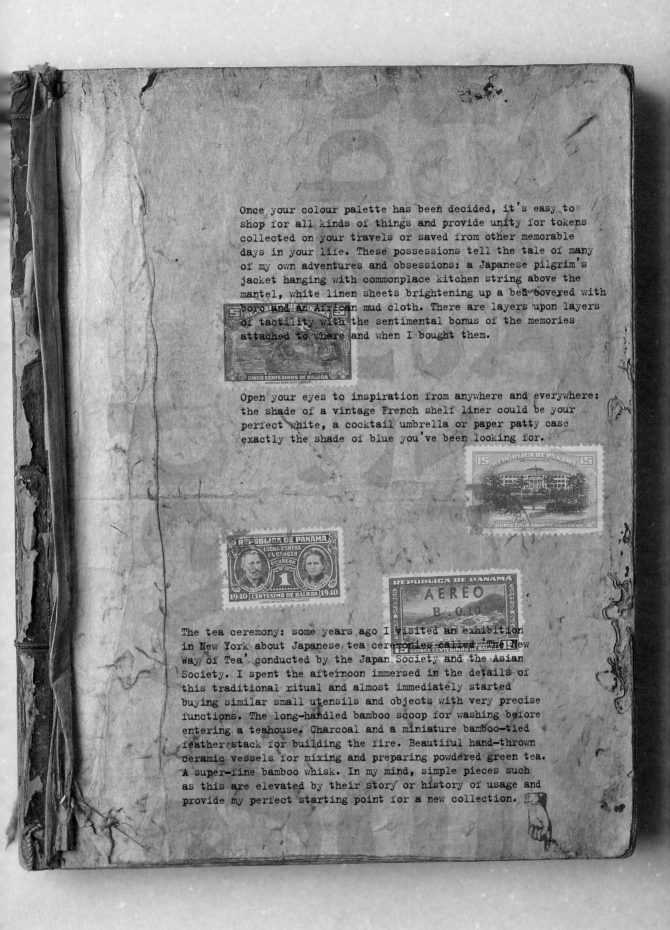

Once your colour palette has been decided, it's easy to
shop for all kinds of things and provide unity for tokens
collected on your travels or saved from other memorable
days in your life. These possessions tell the tale of many
of my own adventures and obsessions: a Japanese pilgrim's
jacket hanging with commonplace kitchen string above the
mantel, white linen sheets brightening up a bed covered with
boro and an African mud cloth. There are layers upon layers
of tactility with the sentimental bonus of the memories
attached to where and when I bought them.

Open your eyes to inspiration from anywhere and everywhere:
the shade of a vintage French shelf liner could be your
perfect white, a cocktail umbrella or paper patty case
exactly the shade of blue you've been looking for.

The tea ceremony: some years ago I visited an exhibition
in New York about Japanese tea ceremonies called 'The New
Way of Tea' conducted by the Japan Society and the Asian
Society. I spent the afternoon immersed in the details of
this traditional ritual and almost immediately started
buying similar small utensils and objects with very precise
functions. The long-handled bamboo scoop for washing before
entering a teahouse. Charcoal and a miniature bamboo-tied
feather stack for building the fire. Beautiful hand-thrown
ceramic vessels for mixing and preparing powdered green tea.
A super-fine bamboo whisk. In my mind, simple pieces such
as this are elevated by their story or history of usage and
provide my perfect starting point for a new collection.

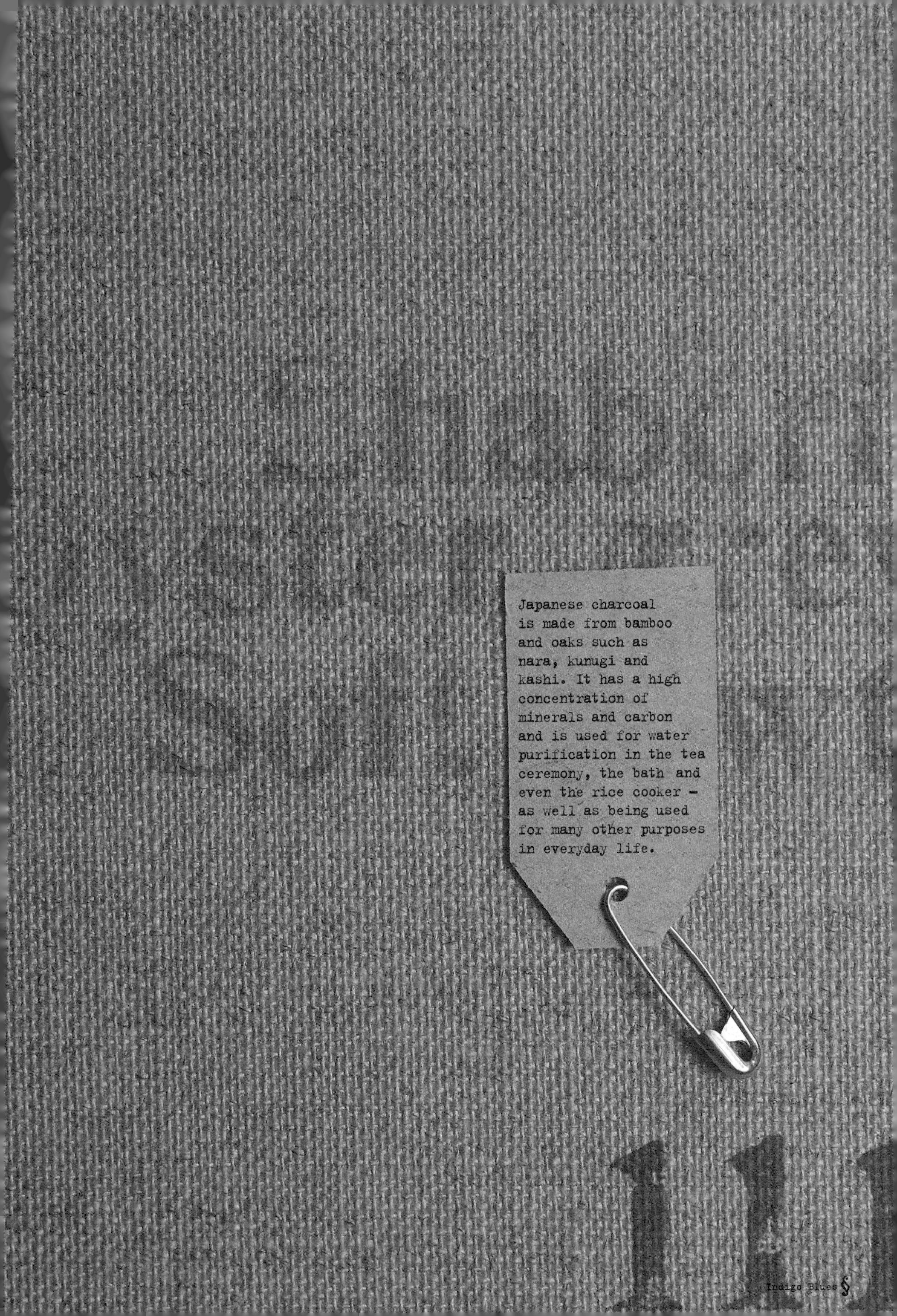

Japanese charcoal
is made from bamboo
and oaks such as
nara, kunugi and
kashi. It has a high
concentration of
minerals and carbon
and is used for water
purification in the tea
ceremony, the bath and
even the rice cooker —
as well as being used
for many other purposes
in everyday life.

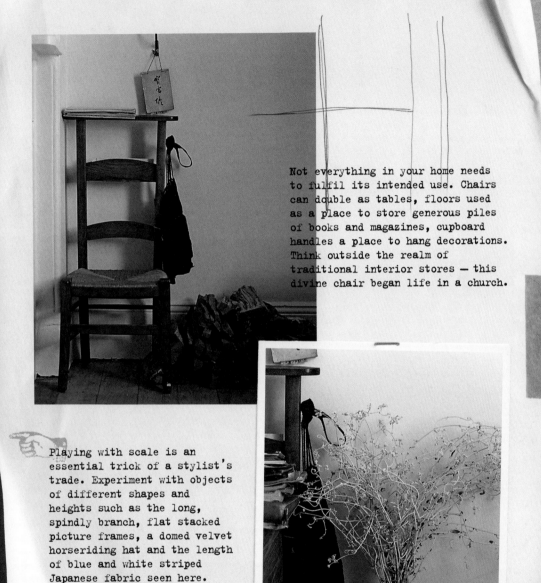

Not everything in your home needs to fulfil its intended use. Chairs can double as tables, floors used as a place to store generous piles of books and magazines, cupboard handles a place to hang decorations. Think outside the realm of traditional interior stores — this divine chair began life in a church.

Playing with scale is an essential trick of a stylist's trade. Experiment with objects of different shapes and heights such as the long, spindly branch, flat stacked picture frames, a domed velvet horseriding hat and the length of blue and white striped Japanese fabric seen here.

Qual. 2365   Lot
Color CAMEL   Yds. 4|
Web.   Width

Wherever I go I find
inspiration and while the
context in which I will use an
object may not be immediately
apparent to me, I never let
something I love pass me by.
Here is a collection of things
I've found over time that
eventually made sense together.
It captures the essence of
Indigo Blues.

It begins with a single
colour, a simple piece
of boro, then come the
variations of blue in this
hand-dyed origami paper. Next
are mussel shells — inky
blue on one side, grey on the
other — which demonstrate
nature's perfect execution of
colour pairings. The shells
then led me to pebbles and
tarnished silver with shades
of grey and a full colour
palette emerges.

Dubbing yourself a collector, whether it be of serious, big budget items or loose-change odds and ends, gives you the perfect excuse to go shopping and forage for new additions to your collections. One of the many things that I hunt for are old scissors.

trav·el·ler — noun
a person or thing that travels.

a person who travels or has
travelled in distant places or
foreign lands.

ma·gi·cian — noun
an entertainer who is skilled
in producing illusion by
sleight of hand, deceptive
devices, etc.; conjurer.

a person who is skilled in
magic; sorcerer.

03

Travellers & Magicians

No.1 Amulet

No.2 Nomad

No.3 Ikat

No.4 Desert

No.5 Moustache

No.6 Samarkand

No.7 Caravanserai

No.8 Aral sea

No.9 Oasis

No.10 Attar of rose

TRAVELLERS & MAGICIANS SPEAKS VOLUMES OF MY MUSINGS
AND IMAGININGS WHEN PLANNING A PHOTO SHOOT OR
DECORATING A SPACE. ONE DAY I'M TRANSPORTED BACK IN
TIME TO A FAMOUS AND REVOLUTIONARY DANCE COMPANY IN
PARIS, THE NEXT I'M FLYING THROUGH THE SKIES ON THE
WINGS OF A NATIVE BIRD OR DRAWING ON MY OWN REAL-
LIFE, GLOBETROTTING ADVENTURES. EVENTUALLY, MY WORLD
OF MAKE-BELIEVE BECOMES A REALITY AND A NEW COLOUR
PALETTE AND STYLING THEME EMERGES.

NO.1

THE BALLETS RUSSES

For years I have been poring over the catalogue from the exhibition
'From Studio to Stage: Costumes & Designs from the Russian Ballet
in the Australian National Gallery'(1990) The colours! The designs!
The controversy! It's all so provocative I can't help but think
in exclamation points! It all began in the early 20th century
when the visionary Serge Diaghilev oversaw the Paris-based Ballets
Russes, and radically merged dance with other creative forces such
as costume and set design, and music. His collaborators included
Matisse, Picasso, and Stravinsky, and other avant-garde artists —
the results were thrilling.
    Imagine the props and paraphernalia that would have been found
backstage at this famous, world-travelling dance troupe: old metal
fringing, swathes of threadbare velvet and heavy brocade curtains,
burlap-covered love seats, oversized papier-mâché props, masks and
animal costumes, sequins, beads and crystals the colour of jewels,
carnival light bulbs, ribbon and silk cord, and painted backdrops.

BIRDS OF A FEATHER

Of all the elements of nature that excite me, birds are very
high up on the list. Well, more precisely, feathers. Give me
a few hours to leaf through an ornithologist's handbook and
my mind is a mosaic of colour and pattern. Let me wander the
halls of a natural history museum to get up close to all kinds
of winged beauties in their taxidermied state (strangely, I'm
particularly drawn to the paper identification tags around their
feet) and my wonderment never ceases.

Some birds are bestowed with many feathers of distinctly
different colours, while other birds have feathers with
oh-so subtle variations that come together to form an intricate
pattern. I love to see high-contrasting underwings and banded,
mottled, or vermiculated breasts and tails, and am ecstatic
when I stumble across a colour combination that, by traditional
interior decorating standards, would seem ludicrous but which
all of a sudden makes perfect sense.

Before settling on the final palette for Travellers &
Magicians I spent the day at the Australian Museum in Sydney. I
was drawn to the plumage of various species of Australian parrot
– Paradise, Double-eyed Fig, Eastern Rosella, and Scaly-Breasted
Lorikeet – but it was the Mistletoebird, with its scarlet chin
and jet black plumage, which got the best of me and lent many of
its colours to the final palette.

FARAWAY LANDS

Every stamp in my passport is evidence of an adventure or memory.
The trips I took all over Asia with my mother hold special
significance because they opened me to a world of mysticism, chaos
and unadulterated colour.

I fell in love with everything that filled the markets
along the old Silk Road, the ancient route of merchants. The
extraordinary natural dyed and handcrafted textiles included horse-
trapping woven trim, embroidered shawls, heavy velvet jackets, silk
and wool rugs, as well as magnificent embroidered suzanis, and the
ikat weaving of Central Asia. There were enamel bowls and plates,
spices, all kinds of talismans, fruit and vegetables, perfumes and
jewels, trinkets for everyday life and special occasions.

I wonder about these bazaars in the days when the traders
would traverse the land with their wares. I think of the amazing
kaleidoscopic sight travellers would have made arriving into
a caravanserai set against the desert oasis backdrop of dusty
yellow, palm greens, and turquoise tiles. I think of the poem by
James Elroy Flecker, 'The Road to Samarkand', which was read at my
mother's funeral. Imagine some of the characters you would have
met: fortune tellers, puppeteers, knife throwers, camel drivers,
letter writers and story tellers, caravan menders, tin smiths,
gypsies and shamans, gold merchants, dance troupes and acrobats,
falconers, and pilgrims.

Rather than letting go of these enchanting visual landscapes
and stories of faraway places, Travellers & Magicians is brought
to life in a 10-Colour-Palette and rich selection of styling ideas.

Every culture has its mystical symbols, but
it's the amulets and talismans of Uzbekistan
that charm me most. In the bazaars, amongst
the produce, cooking utensils, clothes and
furniture, gypsy women sell objects that protect
you, your family, animals, land or home against
the evil eye. Amongst other things are wolves'
teeth and paws, kohl for the eyes, glass beads,
silver Timoride coins, chillies (both dried and
plastic), strings of cloves, human and animal
hair, mirrors, sewing needles, and feathers.
I've scattered a selection on the tables here
to enrich and add meaning to the space.

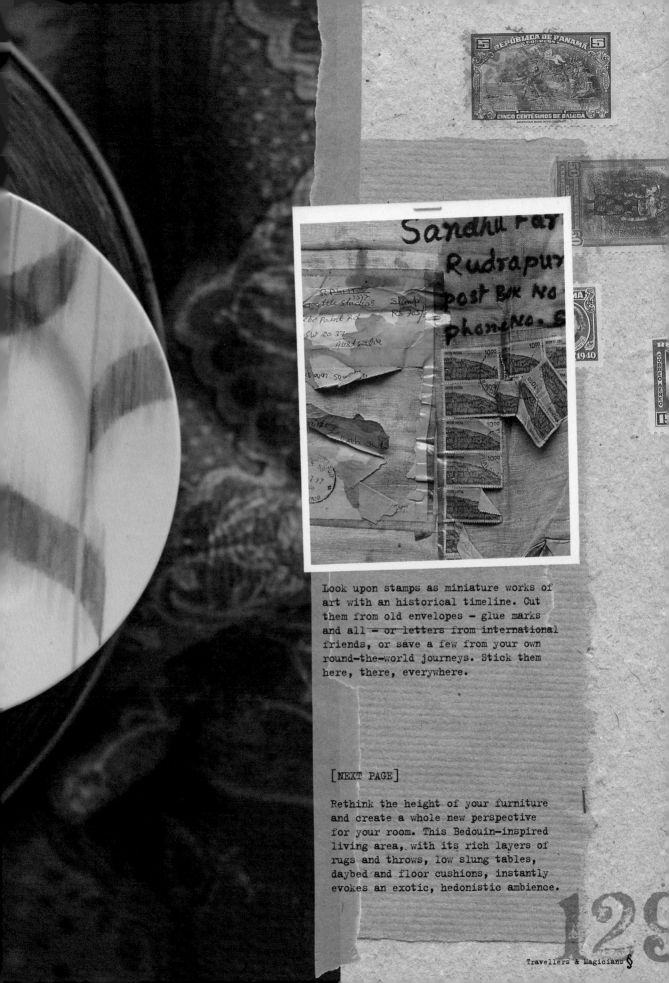

Look upon stamps as miniature works of art with an historical timeline. Cut them from old envelopes — glue marks and all — or letters from international friends, or save a few from your own round-the-world journeys. Stick them here, there, everywhere.

[NEXT PAGE]

Rethink the height of your furniture and create a whole new perspective for your room. This Bedouin-inspired living area, with its rich layers of rugs and throws, low slung tables, daybed and floor cushions, instantly evokes an exotic, hedonistic ambience.

129

Snapshots taken on overseas adventures should be
more than just a record of places you visited.
I took this photo at the Summer Palace in
Bukhara, Uzbekistan, and constantly refer to
it for inspiration: the rich and layered colour
combinations, the textures and shapes on the
walls and floor, and the furniture placement all
have the potential to be part of my own living
space. Flick through your old albums and see what
interiors and architecture took your fancy, then
try to find a way to introduce those
elements into your home.

Upholstery fabrics are rich v
the usual hard and soft furni
of sumptuous velvet can be u
or as a backdrop for other ar
approach with frames – if yo
pictures or artwork to fill th
fabric or exquisite pieces of v

134 Incorporating a quote o
poem or song into your
the space. Use a paint p
less permanent, a penci
and imperfections – it i:
decoration uniquely you

possibilities beyond
coverings. A length
d as a wall covering
ork. Take a similar
haven't yet found the
, use plain or patterned
apping paper.

he words of a favourite
terior instantly personalises
, or if you'd rather something
Don't fret about mistakes
hese that make this kind of
s.

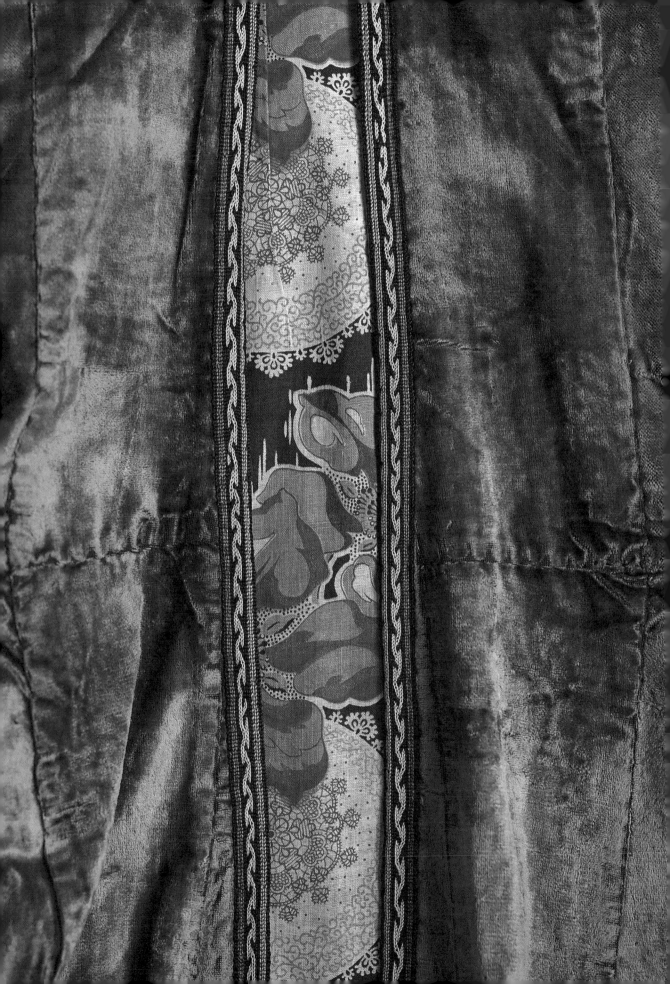

Refining a colour palette can be as simple as
looking at the things you already own and love.
I was drawn to the intense green of this velvet
jacket but also love the way in which the pale
base of the patterned, printed cotton acts as a
neutralising force.

s and viels, And brooderies of intricate design, And

The history of objects is often as important
as the visual beauty they add to a room. A
display of books and odds and ends such as this
invites friends to poke around, pick things up,
ask questions and find out a little more about
you (rather than where you go to shop). Try
an arrangement such as this on your mantel or
somewhere unexpected, such as the table at your
next party.

Every interior should have pieces, such as this
large scale carnivale letter embellished with
multi-coloured Christmas lights, which inject a
sense of humour.

[NEXT PAGE]

Paint instantly changes the mood of a room and the
bolder the colour choice, the more dramatic the
transformation. And the beauty of paint: if you
don't like it or tire of it, you can start all
over again.

If you're feeling super-confident with a paint
brush, try a two-tone wall. The fine, hand-painted
stripe adds another level of interest.

One of the simplest ways to introduce depth to your
interiors is to layer, layer, layer. Textiles, in
particular, offer a tactile and visual beauty like
no other and, when unified by a central colour
palette, a vehicle for dynamic mixture of patterns.

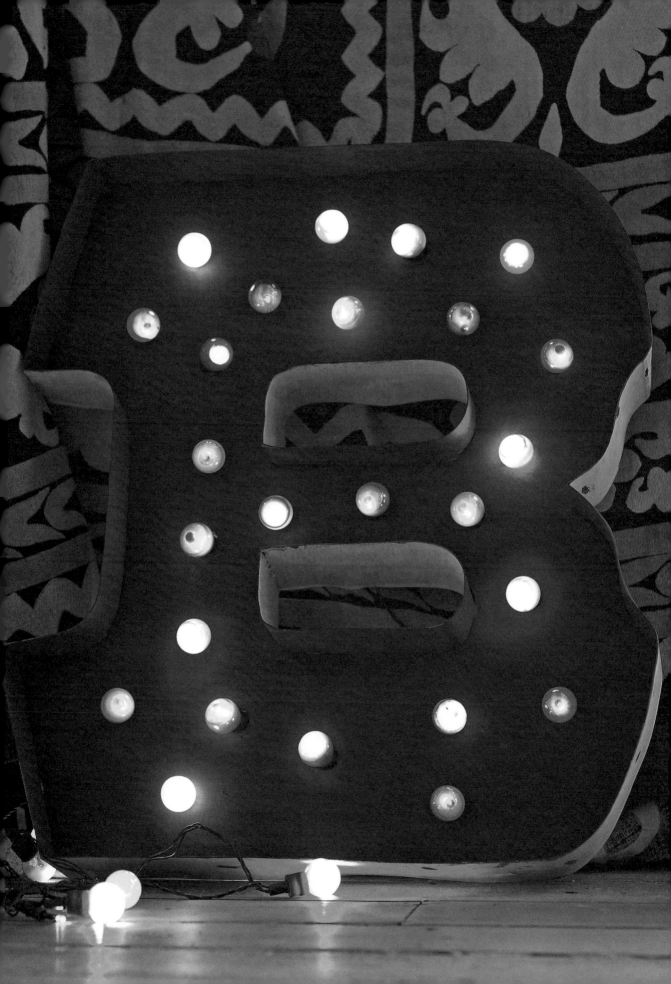

My mother specialised in Islamic textiles from central
Asia, although her love of textiles started with a
simple indigo hill-tribe piece that she unearthed in
Thailand. She travelled the world in search of knowledge
and would return home laden with items of extraordinary
colour, craftsmanship and history: antique turban
fabric, central Asian silks and cotton suzanis, ikat
jackets, vintage cotton Russian prints, dragon print
linen, Indian ralli quilts and so much more. I use this
collection of hers as a constant reference for colour
combinations and design.

A bulletin board of photos taken on holidays or outings around your own home serves as a reminder of the things you love. Use it as a starting point for colour and textural ideas.

Create a collage of paper souvenirs on a horizontal surface as a visual treat for the eyes to rest upon on the way through to another room.

Before you begin decorating, take time to view the space from all vantage points and open and close doors and windows to give you a complete picture of the room and any adjoining areas. Then, when you begin styling and decorating you can place things appropriately and introduce transitional elements – a similar tone, pattern or prop – from one room to the next. In this space, the choice of colours of the front room echoes the suzani on the far wall of the next room.

While travelling in Morocco on a travel story I was invited to a private house for a party. The house was a beautifully built mini kazbah. Jewels on the ceiling, sumptuous silks hanging on floor lamps, pools like rivers snaking around the gardens. But, my most vivid memory, after removing my shoes at the door, was the feel underfoot of layers and layers of rugs. It was spongy and luxurious and quite decadent. I've since copied the look many times, enjoying the sensual feeling it creates.

I'm one for making do with what's in front of me so when I inherited some oddly placed picture hooks, rather than remove them I draped the wall with a giant inky green mosquito net to create a luscious backdrop.

Flowers are a stylist's dream — I love fresh, fabric,
milliner's, and all sorts of printed and artistic
renderings — as the combinations are endless and almost
impossible to mismatch. Experiment with your own floral
motifs and see where it takes you.

Random placement of lighting is an eccentric styling
option. This painted, second-hand shade encloses you
within a shaft of light to make a great reading spot.

[NEXT PAGE]

For all the bits and pieces I gather while out
shopping, walking or on location, my style philosophy
could almost be called 'lost and found'. Feathers are
one of the things I spot with a vengeance. This yellow
South American parrot feather seemed perfectly at home
casually placed next to a velvet tasselled purse and
ancient beads.

EVIL-EYE PROTECTION

NO. 10
NO. 9
NO. 8
NO. 7
NO. 6
NO. 5
NO. 4
NO. 3
NO. 2
NO. 1

Wolves teeth & paws
Kohl for the eyes (also wards
    against infection)
Strings of cloves
Bees waxy honeycomb
Silver Timoride coins
Human hair
Sewing needles
Animal fur
Chillies both dried & plastic
Glass beads

feathers etc.

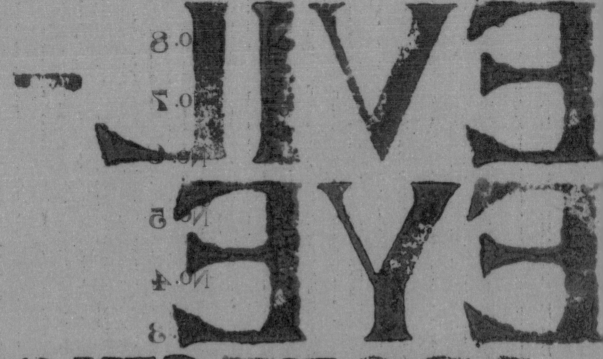

No. 8
No. 7
No. 6
No. 5
No. 4
No. 3
No. 2
No. 1

Glass beads
Chillies both dried & plastic
Animal fur
Sewing needles
Human hair
Silver Timoride coins
Bees waxy honeycomb
Strings of cloves
Kohl for the eyes (also wards against infection)
Wolves teeth & paws

feathers etc.

The artisans who imagined and executed the
extraordinary tiling on the palaces in Samarkand had
a true gift. I could look for hours at the colour
pairings and patterns, in particular the turquoise
minaret — a visual exclamation point like no other.

Loose hanging arrangements allow you to add different
shapes, objects and frames — whatever takes your fancy
— and ensure your rooms can be easily transformed
when the mood strikes.

Paperwhites

04

pa•per — noun
a substance made from wood
pulp, rags, straw, or other
fibrous material, usually
in thin sheets, used to
bear writing or printing,
for wrapping things, etc.

white•s — adjective
of the colour of pure snow,
of the margins of this page,
etc.; reflecting nearly all
the rays of sunlight or a
similar light.

NO. 1   Whalebone

NO. 2   Onionskin

NO. 3   Nautilus

NO. 4   Talas

NO. 5   Moonshadow

NO. 6   Seagull

NO. 7   Loveletter

NO. 8   Dusk

NO. 9   Crepe papier

NO. 10   Seaurchin

WHEN I WAS YOUNG MY PARENTS WOULD TRAVEL TO HONG KONG A
LOT, OFTEN AROUND MY BIRTHDAY. THEY WOULD LEAVE ME THE MOST
FANTASTIC PRESENTS, ALWAYS SMALL AND INDIVIDUALLY WRAPPED;
IT WAS A TRADITION THAT REMAINED ALL MY MOTHER'S LIFE. THEY
WOULD RETURN FROM THEIR TRIPS WITH EVEN MORE TREASURES. MUM
BROUGHT ME SEQUINS AND BEADS FROM ALL OVER THE WORLD WHICH I
LIKED TO SPILL ON THE FLOOR AND SORT BY COLOUR AND SHAPE AND
GROUP WITH MY SHELL COLLECTION.

IT WAS AN OBSESSION WITH SHINY, PRETTY THINGS THAT HAS NEVER
LEFT ME. THIS RITUAL OF OPENING A TREASURE CHEST IS ONE THAT
I HAVE BEEN PERFECTING EVER SINCE. THESE DAYS THE CHEST COMES
IN THE FORM OF THE MULTITUDE OF SMALL CARDBOARD BOXES I OWN,
FILLED WITH ODDITIES AND PRECIOUS NOTIONS. PAPERWHITES IS JUST
ONE OF THE THEMES THAT EMERGE FROM THESE THREE-DIMENSIONAL
SCRAPBOOKS, A MERGING OF COLOURS AND THINGS I LOVE.

WORKS ON PAPER

I first heard the word 'paperwhites' from a photographer friend
of mine. It caught my imagination and, while I'd been a long-
time admirer of paper, I started looking more closely at all
its tones and finishes, from reams of standard snow white copy
paper to gorgeous crepe, onionskin, glassine, vellum, tissue, and
tracing varieties. I then started to consider the hallmarks of
age on paper, especially the muted, stained and faded tones of
ephemera I'd collected over the years: postcards, love letters,
certificates, shelf liners, doilies, patty pans, the backs of
botanical plates, flashcards, wrapped sugar cubes, and matchbooks.
The palette and textures that began to emerge were wonderful.
     Not content with just owning paper for the sheer beauty of it,
and typical of my desire to learn the story behind everything I
love, I went in search of knowledge to feed my obsession. Talas, a
bookbinding supply store, and the Center for Book Arts in New York
were soon two of my favourite places to visit and I began enrolling
in the courses offered by the latter. Learning the book making
skills of folding, printmaking, letterpressing, sewing, glueing,
binding and more, has opened a world of possibilities for styling
and displaying memorabilia and given me a keener eye when searching
for unique pieces for decorating.

FINDERS, KEEPERS

My first memory of collecting goes something like this: I was three
or four, wearing pink bikini bottoms with navy and white ties, and
down on my hands and knees beachcombing the sandbar for beautiful
kelp shells which washed up in huge rifts. They were all shades
of pink from dusty grosgrain to rich aubergine, patterned with
stripes, zigzags and solids. I was always very particular about the
ones I chose as my skin tanned to a very dark shade of brown. Even
then I liked everything to coordinate!

I would then take home the shells and find places to store
them. Each year in my Santa sack (or in my house, pillowcase),
I would receive a jar of Bo-Peeps, the hard jewel-coloured boiled
lollies from Darrell Lea; they came in clear, hourglass bottles
with coloured tops, the perfect size and shape for my kelp
shell collection.

Now, more than thirty years on, my attraction to shells has not
waned. I have boxes and jars, shelves and baskets filled with sea
urchin quills, sand dollars collected from Little St Simon Island,
Georgia, ghost nautilus, and more and more kelp shells.

When I returned to Australia after living in New York for
many years, all I wanted to do was be at the beach, bodysurfing,
sailing, swimming, sunbaking, finding more shells — anything to
experience sunshine, soft breezes, and the open space of our
coastline. It was also December, the festive time of baubles
and trims. Paperwhites began its metamorphosis from there, a
celebration of my love of a summer Christmas.

HUNTER & COLLECTOR

There's another shop I love in NYC called Hyman Hendler & Sons. It
sells vintage French ribbons: each time I go there I leave with a
brown paper bag full of the loveliest of lovely ribbons. I notice
that on different days I am attracted to different colours — but
never random, always a complementary palette.

This is typical of the way I shop and typical of how my mind
works when I'm constructing a new theme or colour palette for
The Society Inc. or my own home. I become completely, supremely
and utterly fixated and wherever I go I'm in search mode. Gallery
and souvenir shops, second-hand stores and antique markets,
close to home or far away, I'm always on the lookout and referring
to my mental list of things I need to buy. My preoccupations
last different lengths of time, often years but sometimes only
weeks, and I end up with collections both full-blown or small
and discreet.

Recently, I had an eye for vintage mother-of-pearl. I found
beautiful Japanese spoons for a fancy miniature entrée, fairy
knives with pearly handles, a set of cocktail napkin rings with
clusters of pearlescent shells, and carved cocktail picks all the
prettiest of colours with a soft shimmer and glow. All spoke of
gentility and etiquette, and the romance of another time, and all
worked within the Paperwhites theme I was dreaming up.

[.....an eclectic mix of
old and new, art, objects,
textiles and furniture

At first glance this is a random selection of
shiny, pretty things — shell clustered napkin
rings, soft milliner's flower, bevelled mirror,
various utensils in opalescent mother-of-pearl,
assorted shells and sea urchins — but for the
stylist in me it represents the starting point
of a colour and decorating scheme. When
developing your own interior style, begin your
own collection of assorted goodies and regularly
sort them into like-minded piles — you'll soon
discover a pattern emerging and start hatching
plans for bigger ideas.

Inspiration

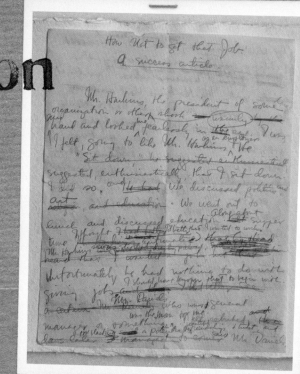

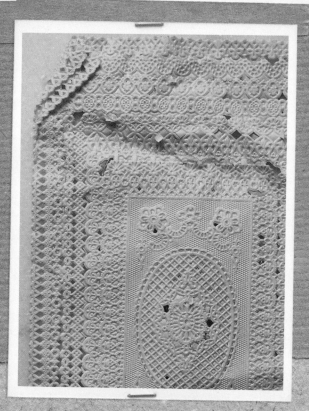

[PREVIOUS PAGE]

For me, holidays are a source of countless hunting and gathering opportunities. As a shell lover, the beach provides me with opportunities to find unique beauties such as sand dollars (which house miniature fairy wings), angels' wings, driftwood and sea urchin quills. Consider your own collections before you go shopping or travelling and you will soon find yourself fossicking for wonderful pieces for your home.

As computers and electronic messaging take over our lives more and more, it's lovely to be reminded of the quirks and imperfections of handwritten letters and notes. This one, titled 'How not to get that job: a success article' and full of crisscrossing and editing marks, was unearthed in a New York flea market, but you might find that your own family archives are full of written memorabilia ideal for framing or displaying.

The intricate embossing and delicate patterns of vintage paper doilies may lead you to possibilities of fine laces, tulle and hand embroidered fabrics, while the creases in the paper echo stiff, crushed linens.

One of my favourite shops in Paris is Fauchon, not only for its tea and edible treats but for its exquisite signature-pink packaging, as seen on these sugar cube wrappers. Keep your eyes open for similarly conceived branded material from retailers and manufacturers both past and present — the colours and graphics may be perfect unto themselves and worthy of display or they may sow a style seedling in your mind.

The wallpaper and fabrics chosen here are unified by a soft, muted colour palette, metallic finishes and sequin and bead embellishments, but the texturally opposite choice of burlap for the chaise longue and the fine, crisp white curtain take the edge of the glitziness.

174

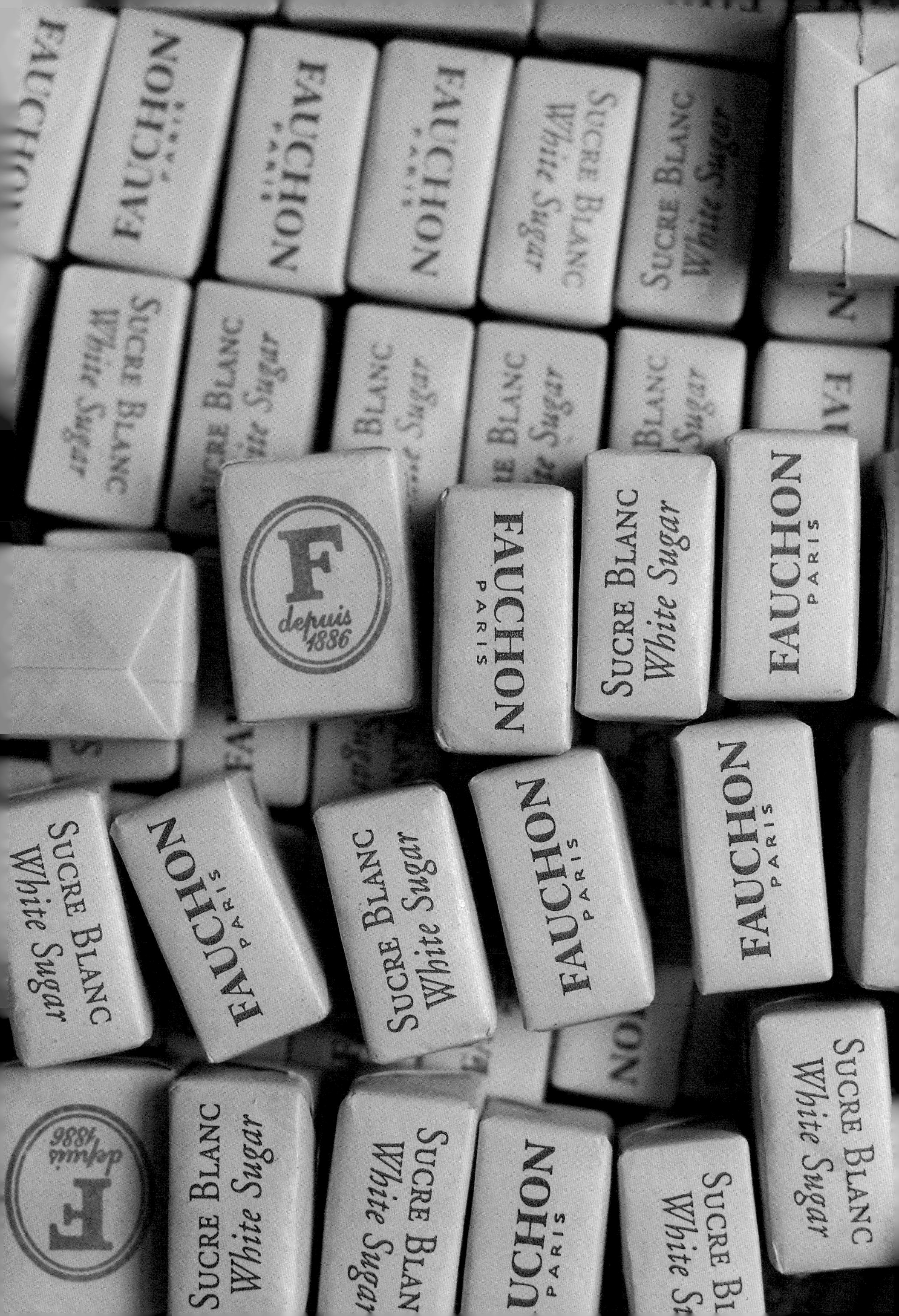
FAUCHON
PARIS
SUCRE BLANC
White Sugar
F
depuis
1886

Crepe
Onionskin
Pattern
Brown self-stripe
Flashcard
Tissue

PAPER & SHELLS I LOVE

Paper Nautilus
Chinaman's Fingernails
Ram's Horns
Tiger Eyes
Cuttlefish
Limpets
Coffin Bay Scallop Shells
Mother-of-Pearl

angelwings etc.

Brown self-stripe
Flashcard
Tissue

PAPERS

SHELLS

Paper Nautilus
Chinaman's Fingernails
Ram's Horns
Tiger Eyes
Cuttlefish
Limpets
Coffin Bay Scallop Shells
Mother-of-Pearl

angelwings etc.

My approach to flower arranging is:
if it holds water, consider it a vase.
Seek out old condiment jars and
bottles, antique milk glass, tarnished
silver trophies — the options and
shapes are endless. Also, embrace
haphazard arrangements — it will make
out flowers look like they're fresh
from the garden.

Painting a rug on the floor is :
and unexpected way to transf
Begin by choosing a graphic
a pattern to copy and either d
ground freehand or transfer
(ask the local office supply or
about their large format print
Paint using a semi-gloss or s
paint. As the paint wears and
pattern becomes even more a
when you tire of it you can si
Also, consider an alternative
and paint the lower half only.
come to waist level in a simil
wainscoting. See page 164 for

ramatic
n your space.
t or finding
v it on the
ising a stencil
inting store
r options).
lar durable
eathers the
ealing and
oly start again.
a feature wall
ie paint should
fashion to
example.

[PREVIOUS PAGE]

Tradition would have you place furniture in set
places, but it's always worth breaking the rules
to utilise your space in different ways. Here,
the chaise is set away from the wall, giving you
complete access to the window. A meterage of
velvet acts as a rug while the light and airy
netting offers spatial interest.

Bowls filled with odd assortments of objects,
such as the mermaids' rings and coastal riffraff
seen here, invite your guests to touch and play
and immerse themselves in your environment.

Art comes in many forms and so it pays to use
your imagination when it comes to decorating
your walls. I discovered this fencing mask in
the US, however, I'm sure he's French. I put it
on and can hear his accent. The paper rosette
demonstrates the results of a simple DIY
project. Start playing around with a roll of
stiff brown paper and see what emerges.

[NEXT PAGE]

I'm a big believer in asymmetry and often style
things to embrace the negative space. Mixing
seemingly disparate objects unified by colour
palette — a star garland, leafy wreath, ball of
twine — creates a personalised, meaningful
vignette rather than a 'I bought everything
brand new' vibe.

Significant holidays such as Christmas are a
stylist's dream, the quintessential time to
unleash ideas, unearth objects and have some fun
with ribbon and a hot glue gun. The fireplace has
been filled with porcelain logs and the improvised
'tree' — a spindly felted branch — decked with
porcelain feathers, felt snowflakes, glass swans
and metal butterflies.

I'm always looking for inexpensive and unconventional ways to display my wares and the many hours I've spent scouting flea markets and snooping at sales have thrown up some interesting options. I'm now officially obsessed with cardboard boxes with compartments – the older the better. Who knows what these boxes originally contained, but they now act as specimen boxes for a few of my favourite things: a dried 'honesty' flower picked with my mum; shells collected by my grandparents when they were young and in love; old French fabric; hand-dyed and handmade artificial flowers; and part of my extensive collection of mother-of-pearl shell spoons.

A garland easily constructed using
oversized plastic dots stapled together
demonstrates the impact of transient,
inexpensive decorations.

Surprise and humour are as appreciated in
homewares as anywhere else and these
porcelain cupcake cases instantly represent
fine craftsmanship and whimsy.

Brown sticky tape should be part of
everyone's styling toolkit as it allows for
instant installations, such as this star
fashioned from ribbon, while the tape
itself has its own humble beauty.

When acquiring new things for your home, don't
limit yourself to interior stores. My love of
ribbon, for example, led me to New York's Tinsel
Trading Co, a magical haberdashery filled with
wondrous trims and notions. Search online or in
your own city for similar sewing suppliers and
start some simple craft projects — ribbon tie-
backs for curtains, tassels for light pulls,
rickrack for edging pillowcases, sequins and
beads for trimming.

[NEXT PAGE]

Visualise your interiors as sets where objects,
art and furniture can be moved or interchanged,
and old objects easily moved to make way for
new pieces or a different mood. In this bedroom,
a floating teak Danish bedside table sits
comfortably next to a rustic birch headboard,
next to a mid-20th century designer table. A play
on scale — the oversized porcelain apple and
giant 'S' above the bed — can also give the
interior a sense of fun in an 'Alice in
Wonderland' way.

THERE'S DEFINITELY NO LOGIC TO THIS

Objects stored on open shelving
and flung-open cupboard doors take
on a new appeal when blessed with
a uniformity of colour, because
what's the point of possessing
beautiful and meaningful things
if you can't show them off for
the world to see?

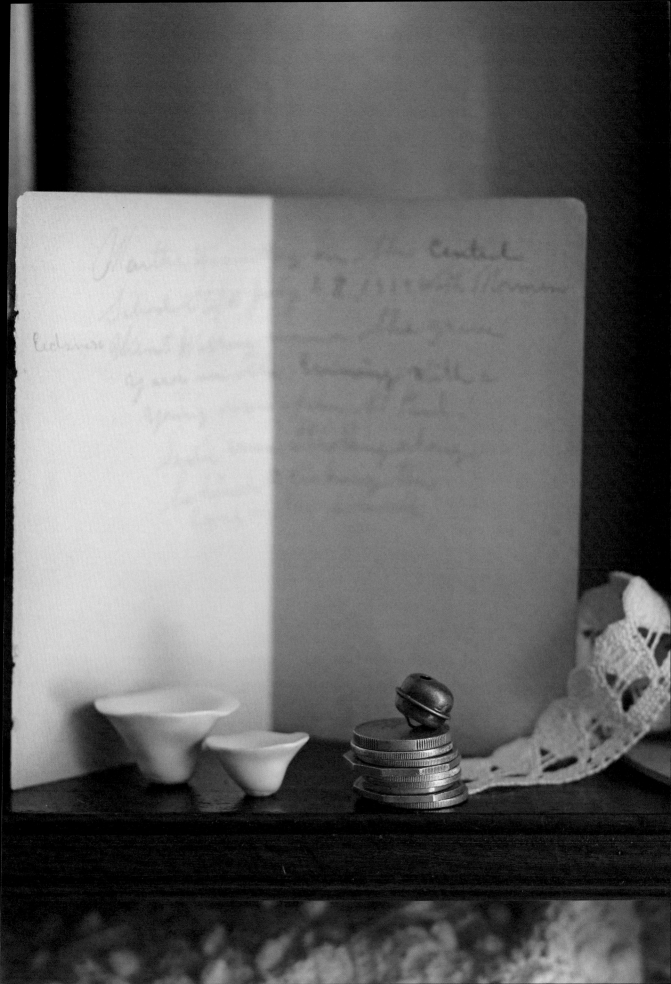

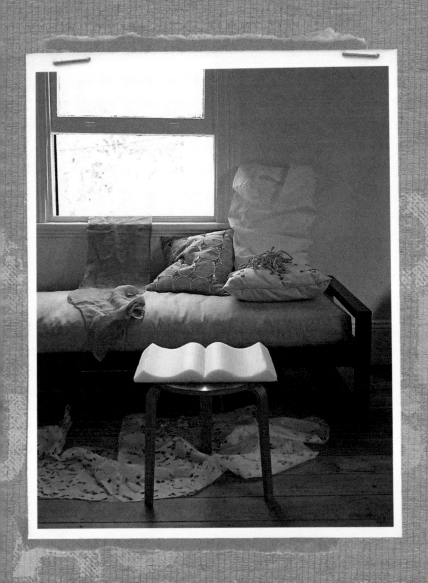

Paperwhites §

[PREVIOUS PAGE]

If you've decided to apply your chosen colour palette
to the entire house, it's important to change the tempo
from room to room, varying the intensity and number of
colours you use. Here, the pinks and dusty purples of the
Paperwhites spectrum have been edited in favour of a few
of the softer, neutral tones. The effect is quiet and
subdued but the addition of the details in the metallic
cushions and cut-out fabric on the floor add texture
and interest.

Improvisation can offer both low budget and remarkable
options for designing a room. In this loose interpretation
of a wardrobe, clothes are hung on the back of an unused
door left leaning against the wall.
The wide steps of the ladder provide shelving, while the
narrower rungs can be used for draping jewellery, scarves
and other accessories.

seventy

trade•wind – noun

also called trades. any of the
nearly constant easterly winds
that dominate most of the tropics
and subtropics throughout the
world, blowing mainly from the
northeast in the Northern
Hemisphere, and from the southeast
in the Southern Hemisphere.

any wind that blows in one regular
course, or continually
in the same direction.

05

Tradewinds

No. 1 Anchorage

No. 2 Seaglass

No. 3 Galleon manila

No. 4 Darwin

No. 5 Wind djinn

No. 6 Galapagos

No. 7 Serpent

No. 8 Tattoo

No. 9 Dark & stormy

No. 10 Whisky

211

TRADEWINDS REFLECTS MY FASCINATION WITH ALL THINGS MARITIME,
FROM THE OCEAN-GOING EXPLORERS OF THE 18TH AND 19TH
CENTURIES TO THE PIRATES AND MYTHOLOGICAL SEA CREATURES OF
STORYBOOKS. IT'S ALSO LITTERED WITH REFERENCES TO ENTOMOLOGY
AND, ONE OF MY HEROES, CHARLES DARWIN. IT IS INSPIRED
BY FACT AND ENHANCED BY FICTION AND HAS A PALETTE THAT,
DEPENDING HOW YOU USE IT, CAN BE EITHER CALM OR WILD, JUST
LIKE THE SEA. AND ME.

NATURAL SELECTION

If I weren't a stylist and shop owner, I'm quite sure I could be
a curator. Everywhere I go, whether the venerable capital cities
of the world or small, non-touristy towns, I seek out museums
and galleries — anywhere that houses a collection. I'm drawn
to anthropology, art and cultural exhibits but feel even more
at home amongst the specimens of birds and bees, flowers and
trees. I could spend days — and have — at the American Natural
History Museum and Sydney University's Macleay Museum but have
also enjoyed many hours at New York's Explorers Club, Oxford
University's Pitts River Museum, and the 178-year-old taxidermy
shop Deyrolle in Paris. I study the beetles, butterflies
cicadas, dragonflies and, of course, my beloved feathered
friends. They all have precise colour combinations and patterns
of such beauty and harmony — it makes my job all the easier.

A long-time love affair with Charles Darwin and his absolute
dedication to collecting, studying and analysing all creatures
great and small has sparked my own interest in the origin of the
species. One thing Darwin and museums inspire in me is the idea
of recording and cataloguing my finds. I love test tubes and
specimen bottles, compartmentalised cardboard boxes with clear
lids, glass domes, and all the methods of entomological pinning
and preservation. I'm intrigued by the meticulous recording of
genus and geographical roots, especially if typed long before
the days of computers. I love handwritten notes and sketches of
flora and fauna done in the field by now-celebrated scientists
and naturalists. These kinds of displays fill me with longing
and desire for the scale and depth of these collections but also
with new ideas for my own cabinets of curiosity.

NO.1

SET SAIL

The Royal Society, the UK's National Academy of Science, has the deliciously suspicious motto 'nullius in verba', which, loosely translated, means 'take nobody's word for it'. That a society could encourage such a renegade and inquisitive spirit instantly makes me wish I was a member. William Dampier - buccaneer, naturalist, cartographer, charter of trade winds - was perhaps too much of a pirate to be accepted by the members of the Royal Society but he dedicated an account of his travels, 'A New Voyage Round the World' (1697), to its president, and Royal Society fellow Charles Darwin described his work as a 'mine of information'.

Just think what Dampier, his crew and other brave seamen would have seen and discovered after endless months on water followed by stints on lands never before heard of. I think of the superstitions of seafarers, the harsh but romantic life of a pirate, stories and songs of wind djinns, sea gypsies, serpents and sirens, weather and wind in all their force and glory, sea creatures and land animals and plants seen and marvelled at for the first time. I'm especially curious about the paraphernalia of a ship's deck: rope, nets, canvas sails, well scrubbed and weathered wood, cleats, pulleys, shackles, figureheads, anchors and chains. And, the names of knots: monkey's fist, figure-of-eight, midshipman's hitch, builder's knot, eight-strand diamond.

READING MATTERS

I think one of the best opening lines in a book is from 'Lighthousekeeping' by Jeannette Winterson. It reads: 'My Mother called me Silver. I was born part precious metal part pirate'. I'm quite sure, despite having never met the author, it was written just for me. It's one of so many examples of words, whether quotes, poetry, fiction or song lyrics, I collect. I write them down, just as people might tear a page from a magazine, to inspire me at a later time or to use in my interiors as artistic embellishment — scribbled on a chalkboard, painted on a wall, mounted in a frame.

The books I read cover many genres, from the magical realism of famous South American writers to childhood favourites by Roald Dahl. I like Oscar Wilde and F. Scott Fitzgerald, books about ships and tales of fantasy. I read fiction and history, and own shelf after shelf of references on photography, travel, textiles and art. Victoria Finlay's 'Colour: Travels Through the Paintbox' is a constant companion. Can't recommend it highly enough.

My collection of books also serves to discredit the maxim 'don't judge a book by its cover'. So many of the ones I own have been bought because of the linen or board with which it's bound, the ribbon bookmarks, or paper stock. Whenever I'm travelling I pick up cheap or second-hand books with unusual fonts or typesetting and especially seek out those with foreign lettering. If they're faded, well-thumbed, or falling apart, well, that's even better. All of them eventually make their way into my home or shop, either as the catalyst for a colour palette or as parts of the many layers of styling.

A friend of The Society Inc. lent me these beautifully-built
bottled boats made by a fisherman from Sydney's northern
beaches. 'Impossible bottling' is rarely seen these days,
which in my mind makes these specimens all the more special.
Keep your eyes open for objects made using dying trades and
crafts like this and you will no doubt be rewarded.

There are so many reasons to amass glass vessels (two of them being the ease and affordability of acquisition) but it's the multitude of shapes that really makes them worth collecting. Look for beakers, bottles, jars, test tubes, goblets, vases, domes, and bowls. Fill and layer them on shelves so everyone can see your collections. The refracting light is a glorious bonus.

Welcome to my cabinet of
curiosities. These customised
floor-to-ceiling shelves,
based on a design I saw in the
glass library of a Venetian
mosaic school, house my
shells, bugs and beautiful
butterflies, feathers, pebbles
and other objet trouvé mixed
in with all kinds of books
and publications. The mini
bay window provides essential
natural light for the dense
display and gives me a lovely
little reading haven.

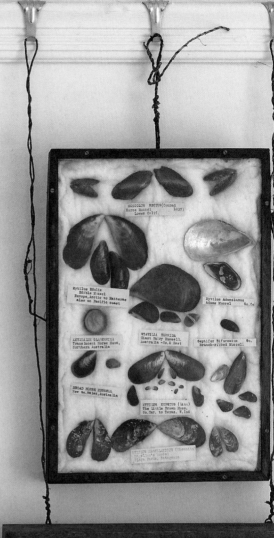

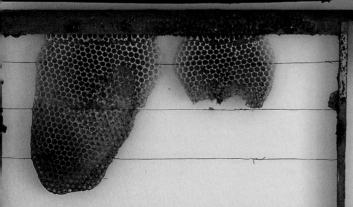

'Up high, down low' hanging arrangements
are an artful alternative to the usual
symmetrical placement. Raffia-wrapped wire,
obviously displayed for all to see, adds
another layer of decoration.

A place for my well-travelled
collection of beach finds
and scientific paraphernalia.
Gazing upon these shelves is
like grown-up eye-spy:

Bird skulls
Leaves
Giant dandelion
Black coral
Dried poppies
Seahorses
Seapods
Petrified wood
Giant cuttlefish
Antlers
Broken stones
Barnacles
Snake vertebra
Dragonflies
Crabclaws
Eggs
Porcupine quills

☞ **Metallics appear in jus**
Palettes and styling t
lustrous tails of mern
the glistening scales o
contrast in texture th
way it picks up and re
in a room. I might use
sprinkling of glitter, a
or sequined embellishn
objects made of precio
silver pieces and table
made of pressed tin or
glass should also be in
enhancing qualities.

bout every one of my 10-Colour-
nes. For Tradewinds it was the
ds and mythical serpents, and
sh that inspired me. I love the
a metallic finish offers and the
ts the light and other colours
int with a hint of shimmer or a
xtile or cushion with a beaded
nt, or perhaps fill shelves with
and everyday metal, decorative
re, or gold-papered boxes, things
ronze. Mirrors and all kinds of
oduced for their wonderful light

A kite in the shape of a pirate ship becomes a mobile held up and roped down with green silk cord. Consider other objects to suspend from ceilings or anchor to floors and encourage your guests to look here, there, and everywhere.

My fascination with the folds and fun of paperboats is incorporated into a still life.

Visual and tactile textures add an important level of interest to any styling arrangement. Here, smooth painted tongue-and-groove is paired with the satiny stiff plumage of a giant seafaring bird; a pebble polished by nature is a companion to twisted cord and fine-grained wood. Note the use of superfine masking tape and dressmakers' pins to affix the feathers to the wall — easy, cheap and effective.

i'm all for brave and surprising uses of colour. The drama of the aquamarine in this setting is enhanced by its imperfect application, the reflective qualities of the dense glass balls and bottle, and the other elements of the oversized still life before it.

§ ETCETERA etc.

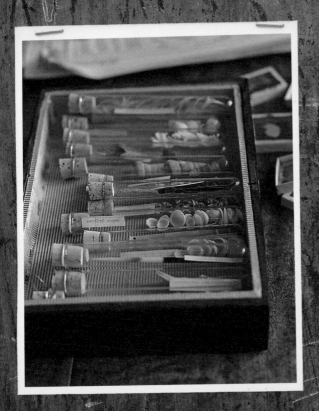

I'm always trying to find new ways to display my finds when getting things ready to go into the cabinet of curiosities. My shells look wonderful placed in a corked test tube with a typed description, sort of scientist-meets-stylist. I've also taken inspiration from entomological cataloguing and made cardboard boxes; pinning and labelling my own amateur finds.

A fixation with pulleys and ropes serves as
more than another excuse for me to rummage
in ship chandleries and seaside antique
stores. I use them at home and in my shop
for many practical reasons — they're perfect
for hanging large items from the ceiling or
wall — but also to add textural differences
or a new focal point.

Small alterations can bring new character
to a piece of furniture. The handles of
these wooden drawers were removed and
replaced with leather thonging bought at
the local shoemaker.

[NEXT PAGE]

To avoid a look that's too prescriptive
it's important to throw something unusual
and unexpected — in this case a taped-up
snapshot and a giant cross made of funeral
foam — into the mix. Also note the old
French linen flour sack in its new life as a
king-size pillowcase; the stripe and texture
make it fit perfectly into the Tradewinds
feel without being too matching.

NO. 10

NO. 9

NO. 8

THINGS I COLLECT

NO. 6

NO. 5

NO. 4

NO. 3

NO. 2

NO. 1

Bird skulls
Paperclips
Pushpins
Matchbooks
Driftwood
Ribbons
Envelopes with string ties
Tendrils
Scissors
Small hammers
Rubberbands
Pulleys
Bones
Amulets
Ribbons
Japanese calligraphy books
Pencils
Tape
Luggage tags & all other tags
Sea sponges
String, rope & thread
Origami paper
Animal quills

ampersands & etc.

THINGS I COLLECT

No.10
No.9
No.8
No.7
No.6
No.5
No.4
No.3
No.2
No.1

Bird skulls
Paperclips
Pushpins
Matchbooks
Driftwood
Ribbons
Envelopes with string ties
Tendrils
Scissors
Small hammers
Rubberbands
Pulleys
Bones
Amulets
Ribbons
Japanese calligraphy books
Pencils
Tape
Luggage tags & all other tags
Sea sponges
String, rope & thread
Origami paper
Animal quills

& ampersands etc.

Inspiration comes in all forms:
a newsletter dating back to 1939
offers a beautiful image that
becomes an embroidered cushion,
custom-made in Bali. The fabric
in the background is an old sail
hanging from a picture hook.

§ ETCETERA etc.

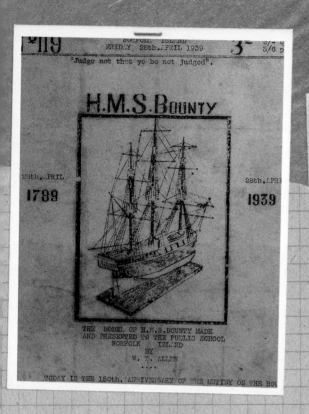

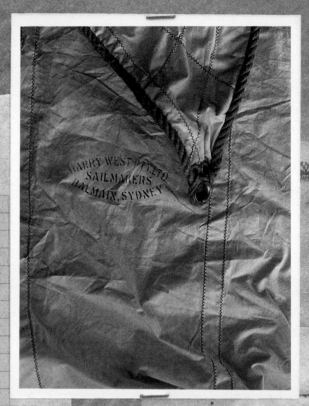

For every theme there is a trail of inspirational clues I follow before I reach a conclusion. For Tradewinds the markers included these favourite things:

A decrepit blue-boxed collection of dragonflies and butterflies found in a Paris flea market.

I arrived at the neutral colours when contemplating the fittings on the boat: decks, brushes, pulleys, rope, ladders, sails, barrels of whisky.

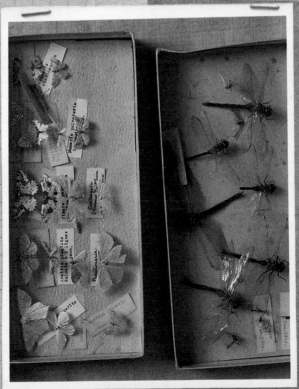

Seaglass and trade beads. Also
evil-eye beads (in so many
shades of blue) — sailors were a
particularly suspicious bunch!

245

When out shopping, pick up the one-off anniversary plate
but please don't display it. Add it to your pile of
tableware and use it at your next dinner party. Embrace
the kitsch and use it for the everyday.

A waxed-twine crochet-covered stone, a petri dish, a
scallop candle, a bone pulley, a cork votive and small
random miniature mop — et voila! — a mini installation
for a side table or window sill.

like anxious folding chairs
i am useless

The intensity and commitment of dark
colour makes a bold and confident
style statement.

The less it matches the more I like
it. Just look at the way these
unusually long-stemmed, late-season
hydrangeas theatrically defy the
proportions of the vase.

My mother called me Silver... part precious metal part pirate.

A pirate flag tied to a chair disguised as a bedside table, next to a faux rock made of felt, in front of vintage wallpaper! Yes, it may sound a little kooky but the principles of styling demonstrated here are very useful. To begin with, it offers simple ideas for taking a piece of furniture rethinking its use. Next, it throws open the possibilities of wallpaper — so many textures and patterns to choose from — not just as a covering for a whole room or feature wall but a creative addition when loosely-erected with pins as freeform art (and, when your styling mood changes you can take it down and use it for something else). The felt rock adds the element of surprise, while the flag, with its multi-faceted shape, height and texture, fills a space in the room that's usually left void.

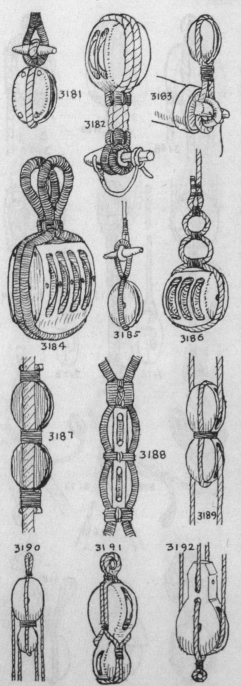

3181. A clew line block is fitted with a toggle. The toggle is buttoned to an eye, termed the clew, in the corner of the sail. It is a very practical method of fitting a block. A similar block is often toggled to pendants for various purposes. If to be left in place for any considerable time, the eye may be closed with a seizing.

3182. The lower block of a *whaler's cutting tackle* is fitted with long double straps which are rove through a hole cut in the blanket piece (blubber), and the toggle is passed through a double thimble.

3183. A *fid block* for a studding-sail tack is toggled to a metal eye in the end of a yard.

3184. A *"heaving-down" block*. The British equivalent would be a "careening" block. I saw what was probably the last merchant ship to be hove down in America. The 384-ton whaling bark *Josephine* was hove down at Merrill's Wharf, New Bedford, in 1893, there being no railway in the neighborhood that could take her, and no drydock available. Peter Black, an ancient master rigger, who in the 1840s had been the last to put the *Constitution* in active commission, resurrected his heaving-down tackle and, with no trouble at all, and much saving of expense, the ship was hove down. She was then breamed, scraped, caulked, payed, sheathed and coppered in record time. The gear he used is pictured on page 530.

3185. A *strap with a* LONG EYE, made with throat seizing ✸3411 was often attached to a pendant bearing a toggle. The same shaped strap was employed in 1808 on lower square-sail sheets. It passed around the necks of the clews, and tacks were buttoned to the clews with TACK KNOTS (✸846).

3186. This method of strapping a *three-shiv block* is given by Vial du Clairbois, in his *Encyclopédie Méthodique Marine* (1787), and it is also given by Roding (1795). It consists of three throat seizings and an end seizing. Nowadays huge blocks such as this are generally strapped as ✸3184.

3187. *Sister blocks.* Two independent tackles, or on occasions one tackle and one bridle, are rove through the two ends of a sister block. This one is scored down one side and is to be seized to a shroud. Shown by Lever (1808).

3188. Sister blocks with scores down both cheeks are seized between two forward shrouds below the topmast crosstrees and are employed for the topsail lift and reef tackle.

3189. In the merchant service sister blocks may have but one shiv, the other end having only a hole which takes a bridle. The strap holds the shiv pin in place. It is hove taut around the shell by a seizing between the two halves.

3190. A *fiddle block* will lie flatter to a yard or mast than a double block will.

3191, 3192. *Shoe blocks* have their shivs at right angles to each other; ✸3191 is eighteenth-century and is double strapped; ✸3192

[524]

seventeenth-century. It is strapped through a hole between the two shivs. Recently shoe blocks have been used for buntlines.

3193. A *lower lift purchase* with standing part strapped to the block.

3194. Two straps may be quickly adjusted to a block in this manner. If there is time they should be seized in.

3195. A CUT SPLICE with single block seized in.

3196. A *pendant block* of about 1600 is shown by R. C. Anderson in his *Treatise on Rigging* (circa 1625).

3197. A *double pendant block* is given by Roding (1795). I do not know its purpose. It may be a fair-leader.

3198. A block from Furttenbach (1629), representative of one of the earliest types known. The standing part is knotted into the breech. The shell is actually a block of wood which, of course, is the origin of the name.

3199. A strap fitted with STOPPER KNOTS from Roding (1795). A lanyard was eye spliced around the neck of one of these STOPPERS and the block was lashed in the rigging just as CABLE STOPPER #1765 is clapped on.

3200. The earliest way of strapping a block was to reeve it through a hole in the upper end of the shell. The method is shown by Furttenbach in 1629. The STOPPER KNOT used at this period would probably be a wall upon a wall (#684).

3201. The early method of strapping, just described, is still employed on snatch blocks. I have one, incised "Bark *America*" on the back, that dates from the first half of the nineteenth century. This method of strapping is also used today on the blocks of tropical jalousies and awning gear.

3202. Quarter blocks are double and have a round seizing. The legs are of equal length, with eyes in each end which lash together over the topgallant yard. The forward shiv takes the topgallant clew line and the after one takes the royal sheet, according to Brady (1841).

3203. A euphroe block has "many holes but no shivers" and is used to extend the edge of an awning.

3204. To strap a reef tackle block: Make a grommet and seize in two thimbles the width of the block apart. Notch the block deeply at the breech and strap in the usual way. Reeve the fall through the two thimbles. The purpose is to prevent reef earings and reef points from fouling in the shivs.

3205, 3206. These are taken from Crescentio's *Nautica Mediterrania* of 1607. Multi-shiv blocks were used to disperse the strain of running rigging that was made fast to the stays. They served a purpose similar to euphroe blocks (see #3276).

3207. This is a threefold block from Roding (1795).

A tackle (pronounced tai'cle at sea) is generally rove in the same

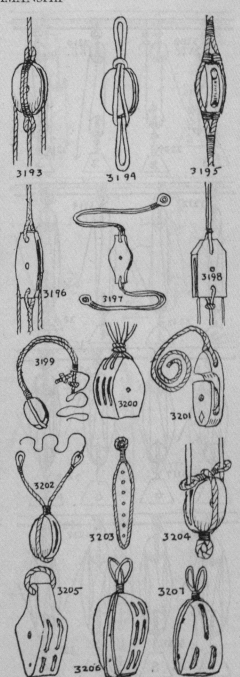

[525]

[AUSTRALIA — SYDNEY]

Sally Campbell
www.sallycampbell.com.au
(vintage & handmade textiles
from India)

grandiflora
112 Macleay Street
Potts Point NSW 2011
Tel: +61 2 9357 7902
grandiflora.net
(flowers)

Major & Tom
45 Barwon Park Road
St Peters NSW 2004
Tel: +61 2 9557 8380
www.majorandtom.com.au
(Australian industrial
furniture & prop rentals)

The Society Inc.
18 Stewart Street
Paddington NSW 2021
Tel: +61 2 9331 1592
www.thesocietyinc.com.au
(textiles, hardware, paint,
homewares)

Doug up on Bourke
901 Bourke Street
Waterloo NSW 2017
Tel: +61 2 9690 0962
www.douguponbourke.com.au
(industrial, commercial, rustic
antiques & collectibles)

Murobond
81 Dickson Avenue
Artarmon NSW 2064
Tel: +61 2 9906 7299
www.murobond.com.au
(boutique decorative paint co.)

Ici et la
7 Nickson Street
Surry Hills NSW 2010
Tel: +61 2 9699 4266
www.icietla.com.au
(French antiques and bits
& pieces)

Reverse garbage
8142 Addison Road
Marrickville NSW 2204
Tel: +61 2 9569 3132
www.reversegarbage.org.au
(recycled supplies from
cardboard to carpet &
everything in between)

Edo Arts
321 Mona Vale Rd
Terrey Hills NSW 2084
Tel: +61 2 9986 1300
www.edoarts.com.au
(Japanese antiques
& collectibles)

Strangetrader
13 Lawson St
Byron Bay NSW 2481
Tel: +61 2 66855888
www.strangetrader.com
(global treasures:jewellery,
textiles, homewares,
furniture)

[AUSTRALIA — MELBOURNE]

Izzi & Popo
258 Ferrars Street
South Melbourne VIC 3205
Tel: +61 3 9696 1771
www.izziandpopo.com.au
(vintage furniture & decorative
pieces)

Guy Mathews Vintage Industrial
Furniture
154 Johnston Street
Fitzroy VIC 3065
Tel: +61 3 9417 5750
(French & European furniture,
lighting & decorative pieces)

A Day on Earth
280 Chapel Street
Prahran VIC 3181
Tel: +61 3 9529 3094
www.adayonearth.com.au
(unusual furniture from around
the world)

Tarlo & Graham
60 Chapel Street
Windsor VIC 3181
Tel: +61 3 9521 2221
(industrial furniture)

Story
4 Wilkes Street
Spitalfields, London E1 6QF
Tel: +44 20 7377 0313
(conceptual space with mix
of homewares & fashion)

Labour and Wait
18 Cheshire Street
London E2 6EH
Tel: +44 20 7729 6253
www.labourandwait.co.uk
(old styled hardware)

Mint
2 North Terrace
London SW3 2BA
www.mintshop.co.uk
(homewares, interior,
artisans)

Alfies Antique Market
13–25 Church Street
Marylebone, London NW8 8DT
Tel: +44 20 7723 6066
www.alfiesantiques.com
(antiques and vintage
treasure trove)

Castle Gibson
106a Upper Street
London N1 1QN
Tel: +44 20 77040927
www.castlegibson.com
(restored furniture &
eclectic one-off pieces)

Margaret Howell
34 Wigmore Street
London W1U 2RS
Tel: +44 20 7009 9009
www.margarethowell.co.uk
(detail driven fashion &
modernist furniture and
homewares)

Paul Smith
22 Kensington Park Road
London W11 2EP
Tel: +44 20 7727 3553
www.paulsmith.co.uk
(fashion & quirky homewares,
decorative bits & pieces)

Dover Street Market
17–18 Dover Street
London W1S 4LT
Tel: +44 20 7518 0680
www.doverstreetmarket.com
(conceptual space showcasing
latest & greatest in fashion
and interior design)

Few and Far
242 Brompton Road
London, SW3 2BB
Tel: +44 20 7225 7070
www.fewandfar.net
(eclectic mix of fab global
homewares)

etc.

[FRANCE — PARIS]

Le Marché aux Puces de la Porte
de Vanves (flea market)
Weekends at Avenue Marc Sangnier
(7am to 1pm) and Avenue Georges
Lafenestre (afternoon), Porte
de Vanves
www.pucesdeparis-portedevanves.com
(French antiques & curiosities)

Marie Papier
26, rue Vavin
75006 Paris
Tel: +33 1 43 26 46 44
www.mariepapier.fr
(beautiful stationery suppliers)

Deyrolle
46, rue du Bac
75007 Paris
Tel: +33 1 42 22 30 07
www.deyrolle.com
(taxidermy & all things
entomological)

Muji
27, rue Saint-Sulpice,
75006 Paris
Tel: +33 1 46 34 01 10
www.muji.com
(Japanese 'basics' for
everyday living)

Caravane
6, rue Pavée
75004 Paris
Tel: +33 1 44 61 04 20
www.caravane.fr
(modern handmade textiles
for the home)

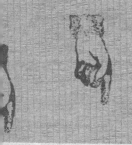

[UNITED STATES – San Francisco]

Tail of the Yak
2632 Ashby Avenue
Berkeley CA 94705
Tel: +1 510841-9891
(unusual homewares & vintage inspired jewellery)

Bell'occchio
10 Brady Street
San Francisco CA 94103
Tel: +1 415 864 4048
www.bellocchio.com
(French collectibles, beauty, home, haberdashery)

Cookin'
339 Divisadero Street
San Francisco CA 94117
Tel: +1 415 861-1854
(everything vintage cookware)

FLAX art & design
1699 Market Street
San Francisco CA 94103
www.flaxart.com
(best art supply store)

Paxton Gate
766 Valencia Street
San Francisco CA 94110
Tel: +1 415 252-9990
www.paxtongate.com
(taxidermy, entomology, plants)

[UNITED STATES – New York]

John Derian Company
6 E 2nd Street
New York, NY 10003
Tel: +1 212 677-3917
www.johnderian.com
(textiles, unusual antiques, stationery, furniture, homewares)

Hyman Hendler & Sons
21 W 38th Street
New York, NY 10018
Tel: +1 212 840-8393
www.hymanhendler.com
(ribbons: old & new)

Paula Rubenstein
65 Prince Street
New York, NY 10012
Tel: +1 212 9668954
(unusual or industrial Americana, homewares, furniture, textiles)

Darr
69 Atlantic Avenue
Brooklyn, NY 11217
Tel: +1 718 797-9733
www.shopdarr.com
(industrial and commercial vintage furniture)

Anthropologie
50 Rockefeller Center
New York, NY 10020
Tel: +1 212 246-0386
www.anthropologie.com
(emporium of home, fashion, gallery)

Talas
330 Morgan Avenue
Brooklyn, NY 11211
Tel: +1 917 237-1618
www.talasonline.com
(bookbinding suppliers)

Tinsel Trading Company
1 W 37th Street
New York, NSW 10018
Tel: +1 212 730-1030
www.tinseltrading.com
(vintage & new ribbons & haberdashery)

ABC Carpet & Home
880 Broadway, NYC
www.abchome.com
(carpets, homewares, fashion)

[WORTHY MUSEUMS]

Deyrolle
46, Rue Bac, 75007 Paris, France
Tel: +33 1 42 22 30 07
www.deyrolle.com

American Natural History Museum
79 Street & Central Park West
New York, NY
Tel: +1 212 769-5100
www.amnh.org

Museum national d'Histoire naturelle
Gallerie de Paleontologie et d'Anatomic Comapree
rue Cuvier, 75005 Paris
Tel: +33 1 40 79 54 48
www.mnhn.fr

Pitt Rivers Museum
South Parks Road
Oxford OX1 3PP
Tel: +44 1865 270927
www.prm.ox.ac.uk

Macleay Museum at the University of Sydney
Gosper Lane off Science Road, NSW 2006, Australia
Tel: +61 2 9351 2274
www.usyd.edu.au/museums/index.shtml

Australian Museum
6 College Street
Sydney NSW 2000, Australia
Tel: +61 2 9320 6000
www.austmus.gov.au

Bellview Shell Museum
Bussell Highway
Witchcliffe WA 6286
Tel: +61 8 9757 6342

Bass Strait Shell Museum
12 Noel Street
Apollo Bay VIC 3233
Tel: +61 3 5237 6395

Thank you

Here's thanks to you for your support, advice, love,
help, encouragement and general greatness to make this
super cool book happen:
Especially to my brother/photographer, Chris Court
My dad, Peter Court
Nicole & Damo Court
Jack Kain
Reuben Crossman
Bianca Spiegel
James Merrell
Katie Dineen
Edwina McCann
Emily McGregor
Donna Hay
Jana Frawley
Kay Scarlett
Katrina O'Brien
Rowena Judd

Varto (my electrician)
Sally campbell
Edo arts: Carman & Paul
Murobond Paints

Published in 2009 by Murdoch Books Pty Limited

Murdoch Books Australia
Pier 8/9
23 Hickson Road
Millers Point NSW 2000
Phone: +61 (0) 2 8220 2000
Fax: +61 (0) 2 8220 2558
www.murdochbooks.com.au

Murdoch Books UK Limited
Erico House, 6th Floor
93-99 Upper Richmond Road
Putney, London SW15 2TG
Phone: +44 (0) 20 8785 5995
Fax: +44 (0) 20 8785 5985
www.murdochbooks.co.uk

Photographer: Chris Court
Designer: Reuben Crossman
Project Editor: Katrina O'Brien
Editor: Jana Frawley
Production: Karen Small and
Elizabeth Malcolm

National Library of Australia
Cataloguing-in-Publication Data

Author: Court, Sibella.
Title: Etcetera: Creating beautiful
interiors with the things you love
/ Sibella Court.
ISBN: 9781741965568 (hbk.)
Subjects: Interior decoration.
Dewey Number: 747

A catalogue record for this book is
available from the British Library.

PRINTED IN CHINA.
Reprinted 2009, 2010 (five times).